JANE ASHER'S
TRICKS OF THE TRADE

HELPFUL HINTS
TO MANAGE
YOUR LIFE

Thorsons
An Imprint of HarperCollins*Publishers*
77–85 Fulham Palace Road,
Hammersmith, London W6 8JB

The Thorsons website address is: www.thorsons.com

Published by Thorsons 1999

10 9 8 7 6 5 4 3 2 1

© Jane Asher 1999

Jane Asher asserts the moral right to
be identified as the author of this work

A catalogue record for this book
is available from the British Library

ISBN 0 7225 3944 4

Printed and bound in Great Britain by
Woolnough Bookbinding Ltd, Irthlingborough, Northants

CONTENTS

ABOUT THE AUTHOR

Jane Asher is a well-known stage and television actress who has also written many successful books. Her first cake decorating book, *Jane Asher's Party Cakes*, was published in 1981, and she has also published two best-selling novels: *The Longing* and *The Question*.

Jane also runs Jane Asher Party Cakes and Sugarcraft, a successful business supplying hand-crafted cakes and specialist sugarcraft equipment. For details of her mail-order cakes for all occasions ring 020 7584 6177 or visit Jane's website on www.jane-asher.co.uk.

ACKNOWLEDGEMENTS

Well, obviously I couldn't have done all this on my own, could I? Anyone who knows without help all the answers to such a strange, varied and at times obscure set of problems is either extremely nerdy or has the retentive memory of an Einstein, in which case he or she would be too busy to write this book. My brilliant researcher Alice Westgate is the lynch pin: all through the year, even in the last weeks of her first pregnancy, she continued to unearth the oddest facts and most unexpected answers and has been the best possible support and friend. My thanks too, to all the people whose brains I have picked for answers, including the wonderful Ruth and David at my shop, assorted friends, family and work colleagues and my long-suffering assistant Julie. Also, of course, to *Express* editor Rosie Boycott for inviting me to join the paper in the first place, and to the patient and extremely helpful editor of this book, Jane Ross-Macdonald.

PREFACE

I began writing a weekly page for the *Express* newspaper about a year ago. My original brief was to tackle mainly cookery questions, but we were taken aback by the amount and variety of the questions that came flooding in, and it soon became clear that we should broaden the range of subjects covered to include as many as possible of the fascinating, unusual and pertinent problems sent in by readers.

Some answers I knew; many I didn't, and over the last year I have learnt a great deal, much of it extremely useful, some of it quite unexpected. The response from readers has been wonderful, and I've particularly enjoyed it when letters have come in to the page offering alternative solutions to other readers' problems or simply additional bits of information or tips: many of these I have included in the answers in this book.

I hope you find the information on these pages as interesting and useful as I and my readers have and that, in any case, you get as much enjoyment out of reading it as I have had in writing it.

Jane

ABOUT THE HOUSE

In spite of all our modern household gadgets and so-called labour-saving devices, housework doesn't seem to get any easier or simpler as the years go by. Maybe it's because we quickly adjust to progress and take it for granted – it can seem very tedious to have to fill and empty the washing machine and tumble dryer, for instance, but when I think back to my mother using a washboard and mangle I remind myself how lucky I am. There are solutions for almost every domestic problem nowadays, from stains to smells, and from broken glass to missing china – it's partly a question of being prepared, and partly of knowing where to look.

Yellow Pages is a good start for finding help, and if you're having trouble with a machine, gadget or appliance don't forget to check the manual, ask the original supplier or ring your largest local department store. Keep a good stock of proprietary cleaners to hand, but remember the value of remedies like vinegar, soda crystals and, of course, soap and hot water. It's only too easy to reach for the nearest sprays instead, but – as well as being expensive and helping to pollute the environment unnecessarily – modern chemicals are often not as effective as old-fashioned methods.

I tend to be a natural hoarder, and my house is full of piles of stuff I mean to go through: a good clear-out every now and then can be very cleansing to the mind. Although our disposable culture tempts us to feel we can just chuck things in the dustbin (I long ago decided life was too short to darn socks), I do try not to waste things that might have some life left in them – almost everything can be cleaned, restored, dyed, mended, adjusted or renovated if you find the right advice, or at the very least be taken to a jumble sale or charity shop so that others may reap the benefit. Look in the *Where Can I Find ...?* section of this book for more ideas on how to track down the help you may need.

Jane Asher's

CLEANING

Q Do you believe in spring-cleaning? My mother was a stickler for emptying every cupboard and drawer at that time of year. I just don't have time as I work long hours and feel rather guilty that the mess and grime must be piling up in every corner. You're busy and I can't imagine you fitting in such chores every spring. Please say it doesn't matter!

A I cheat. Although I shop and cook for the family every day I have lots of help with the other housework; so I'm certainly in no position to criticize anyone for not wanting to clean. I'd love to pretend that my natural instinct is to leap about with a feather duster, but it definitely isn't. I'm writing this surrounded by overflowing cupboards and piles of things waiting to be mended/sorted/put away. I have great sympathy with the writer Quentin Crisp, who discovered that he could live quite happily without ever dusting anything, and my advice is to not feel guilty at all if you can't find the time for a spring clean: wait for a break from work and fit it in when you can.

Q My granny says I should keep vinegar in the house. I don't think she means the balsamic kind – can you enlighten me?

A Vinegar is one of the cheapest and most versatile household fluids, and your granny is right – no home should be without a plentiful supply of the white variety. Before reaching for your corrosive descalers and toxic bleaches, grab a bottle of eco-friendly vinegar. Use a tablespoon in washing-up water to help remove grease from dirty dishes; use it for de-furring kettles and for shining up bathroom tiles. Simmering a strong solution of vinegar and water will remove dark stains from aluminium saucepans, and a weak solution is great for mirrors and windows. Add it to soap powder to dissolve stains in glass vases, and dip hardened paint brushes in hot vinegar to soften them. Repeated applications will even clean lavatories – if you're prepared to spend a long time bending over the bowl . . .

How do you remove candle wax from a carpet?

Remove as much as possible by scraping, then cover with blotting paper and apply a warm iron until all the wax has been absorbed. I've had to do this on clothes and it does work. Be warned, though – if your carpet contains nylon the iron will melt the fibres and you will end up with a hole in the carpet . . .

My daughter has managed to spill nail polish on her carpet. I am worried that if I try to clean it off I'll just make the mark worse.

Try this. Dab on some solvent, then blot. Sponge on some detergent, then blot. Sponge on water and blot until it is (hopefully!) gone. This should work, but if not I suggest you get the professionals in to see to it.

Jane Asher's

Q **How can I remove chewing gum from a stair carpet?**

A There are few things more disgusting than finding someone else's chewing gum stuck somewhere about your person, or around your house. The best solution is to freeze the soiled item and then gradually chip the chewing gum off. Unfortunately for you, your stair carpet can't exactly be shoved in the freezer, so your best bet is to rub the area with an ice cube, and then break the gum off carefully to avoid damaging the carpet.

Q **Left alone for half an hour, my children scribbled with felt tip pen all over my new bedroom wallpaper. I'm furious – will it come off?**

A How upsetting for you that your beloved little ones have immortalized your wallpaper in such a way. I have used a remedy to remove stains from fabrics and carpets which may be worth a try on your wallpaper (obviously try it out on an inconspicuous area first, because I can't guarantee success): sponge it with trichlorethylene and blot dry with a clean cloth. Then use a little detergent on a damp cloth. It just might work.

Q How do I get felt tip pen off fabric?

A Whoever invented felt tips has a lot to answer for: although they are a joy to use – at any age – they must be responsible for more marks on sheets, clothes and walls than any other writing instrument. It's the bright orange one with the cap left off that lets its ink seep slowly but inexorably onto one's best white bed cover that gets me: we used to try banning them at home, but it never quite took. Try dabbing on nail varnish remover, surgical spirit or methylated spirits. Rinse and wash as usual.

Q My children always come home from school with paint marks on their clothes. It doesn't seem to wash out, although I'm told it should.

A With water-based paints you should always rinse and wash the item of clothing straight away; if you leave it until it's dry it won't come off. Try telling that to a keen eight-year-old artist or his harassed teacher, though. Perhaps the only solution is to ask the school to insist on overalls? Incidentally, oil-based paint on clothes should be sponged with white spirit before rinsing and washing as usual.

Q One of my children has got Biro marks on my dark green leather sofa. Have you any idea what would remove it?

Jane Asher's

A Ball point pens and leather sofas don't go well together, it seems. There are a couple of things to try, I am told. One is methylated spirits, first doing a pre-test on an inconspicuous area. I have also heard that a little hair spray rubbed onto the mark with a soft cloth works, as does the acne cream Oxy-10 (I suppose our faces are leather, after all, so it kind of makes sense). Or you could visit somewhere like World of Leather (telephone 0990 604060 for branches) where they sell all sorts of proprietary stain removers and can offer good advice, including where to get hold of a leather repairer.

Q **My girlfriend's golden retriever has taken a shine to my dark green sofa. I don't want to cause a rift by banishing it from the living room, so can you suggest a hassle-free way of removing the dog hairs?**

A Simple. Rub with a wet chamois and the hairs will come away easily.

Q **How can I get wine stains out of white table linen?**

A The best advice I can give you (and it is probably too late) is to act quickly! Mop up as much as you can as soon as the wine is spilt, with salt and paper towels, and soak the area with water. One friend says one should simmer the stained part in milk for 20 minutes – holding it carefully, I imagine.

Q I have a slate floor in my kitchen but I can't get it to shine. As soon as I wash it the surface becomes very dull. It is a new kitchen and though the floor was perfect at first I am now worried that I made the wrong choice.

A We nearly went for a slate floor when we re-did our kitchen but – I hate to tell you – were warned that it can be tricky to look after, so we eventually used a kind of tile that looks like terracotta but isn't. But don't panic: after some enquiries I've been told it's all a question of the right finish. I spoke to Fired Earth (01295 812088) who have supplied many handsome slate floors. It all depends if your floor has already been sealed – if not, then it should be. One or two coats of Fired Earth's Stone Shield will do the job. Follow this up once or twice a year with another product called Stone Finish and the depth of colour will shine through.

Q We have recently moved to a flat that has parquet flooring. I'm not sure how it should be cleaned or polished, so I would appreciate advice on maintaining it.

A Put a dash of mild detergent in a bucket of tepid water, then wipe across the floor with a clean, well-wrung-out mop and leave to dry for a couple of hours. Campbell Marson, a supplier of parquet flooring, produces a special cleaner and a polish that can be applied to keep the floor shiny. Visit the firm at 573 King's Road, London SW6 or call 020 7371 5001 to order it by post.

Q I was fitting some new raspberry-coloured brocade curtains recently, helped by my husband who is a keen DIY enthusiast. While drilling in the fixings he managed to get some oil from the drill bit on the brand new fabric. The curtains hang so as to conceal the stain, but I know it's there.

A Do you think your husband is really cut out for DIY? Meanwhile, don't despair about the oil on the curtains, there's a wonderful man called Alan Rigby in Stockport who knows everything there is to know about cleaning. He suggests that a proprietary solvent should do the trick, releasing the oil without leaving a tide mark as the fluid evaporates. Follow the instructions carefully, testing the solution on a scrap of the fabric first. Or you can let Alan deal with it: ring Rigby Cleaning Services on 0161 431 7845.

Q What should I do about coffee stains on my curtains? Can I get them dry cleaned?

A If you call 0161 432 8754 you will be put in touch with a member of the National Federation of Master Window & General Cleaners in your area, and they in turn will advise you as to the best way to proceed. Dry cleaning won't work, as the stain is water based.

Q Can you please tell me how to clean a self-clean oven that doesn't?

A It depends on what kind of oven you have, as all the models work in different ways. I know this sounds obvious, but have you checked the manual? It might be that you're not using your oven for long enough (usually 2–3 hours) at a high enough temperature for the self-cleaning function to work. It normally does so by carbonizing any food spills, which then drop to the floor ready to be cleaned out. But it's possible that there is a fault, too. Either way, make sure by calling the supplier and asking for specific advice. I've never owned a self-cleaning oven and always thought it sounded too good to be true. Perhaps it is?

Q How can I clean the inside of my microwave oven?

A You may have to scrape off the burnt-on food with a razor blade (obviously very carefully), then use one of the special cleaning solutions designed for ceramic hobs, available from supermarkets.

Q How can I remove water marks from a chrome draining board? Friends who wash up for me (I am disabled) do not wipe it down properly.

A Are you sure it's chrome? Most draining boards are polished stainless steel from which hard water deposits can be removed with products such as Scrub Brite by Armway (£3.87 for 500 ml; call 01908 363184 for distributors) or Viakal (£3.99 from B & Q). For everyday wiping I suggest you keep a bottle of any stainless steel/ceramic hob cleaner near the sink and tactfully persuade your friends to add a bit to the cloth when they wipe down.

Q How can I clean my roasting pans? They are so gummed up and encrusted I am wondering whether to throw them away. Brillo pads don't seem to work.

A Many people make the mistake of using too much water with Brillo pads, which rather defeats the object as the cleaning agents within them are rinsed away. Try this: rinse the pan with warm water and pour it away. Just dampen the Brillo pad in a little warm water and scrub the pan with it. Rinse again and repeat the same process. You may need to use more than one Brillo to get the pan really clean, but it's certainly cheaper than buying new roasting pans.

Q My daughter's chest freezer was accidentally turned off, and on opening it she found that everything had gone rotten and the smell was appalling. After disposing of the contents on the council tip, she cleaned it out several times – but no good! She filled it up with bicarb and had another scrub, but it still smells. I phoned a freezer shop and all they could say was 'get an engineer in.' Please, have you any suggestions?

A This is worth a try. With the freezer turned off, use some special fridge/freezer cleaner (Lakeland Plastics, 01539 488100, do one for £4.95) or a solution of Milton (babybottle sterilizer, available from supermarkets) to wipe out every nook and cranny of the freezer's interior. This should kill any of the bacteria that are causing the smell. Let it all dry, then fill the freezer with crunched-up sheets of newspaper and leave it like this for three or four days with the door open; any remaining smell should vanish.

Q **I'd rather not chuck bleach down my drains to keep them fresh – is there something else that would do the job and not harm the environment?**

A Good old bicarbonate of soda has lots of household uses, one of which is to wash a couple of tablespoonfuls down your drain every so often. It is also good for cleaning ovens, stainless steel, and getting rid of tea and coffee stains on cups. And while we're on the subject of drains, don't throw your coffee grounds in the bin; they should go down your sink where they will help dissolve grease.

Q **I have a marble floor in my kitchen and I know I should be careful with it – do you have any advice?**

A Clean it with a damp cloth and a mild detergent. Marble is porous so don't let it get too wet or leave spilt fluids on it for long. If it is a very special floor you might be well advised to get hold of a marble cleaning kit from UK Marble, on 01432 352178.

Q

I find it almost impossible to keep my ceramic sink white.

Once a week, fill your sink with hot water and bleach and leave for an hour – that should do the trick.

Q

I have been putting wine glasses in the dishwasher and, at first, they came out sparkling; now they're only fit for the bin – they have gone dull and cloudy with streaks on them. I've tried several remedies suggested by friends (vinegar, lemon juice, putting them through a cycle with a special cleaner) but nothing has worked. Should I not use the dishwasher for glasses?

I assume that you've checked the salt in the machine if you're in a hard-water area, and that you've plenty of rinse-aid in it. If so, then I'm afraid your glasses are not dishwasher safe. Crystal glasses, for instance, should always be washed by hand, other-wise the damage you describe – known as etching – is bound to happen. It is, sadly, permanent, say the glass experts I spoke to at Thomas Goode. Check in the dishwasher manual about other glassware.

Q I'm fuming because I have just bought some new wine glasses and when I tried to peel off the numerous price labels and product code labels that were stuck on to them, they all left behind a horrid sticky mess that makes the whole set unusable. Are the glasses ruined or can they be rescued for use at the house-warming party we are planning?

A I've just had exactly the same problem: some tumblers I bought last week had three labels on each, which did seem excessive. The proliferation of sticky bits of information on everything we buy drives me wild: particularly on food. If you don't want to bother to take your wine glasses back and complain, then try 'Sticky Stuff Remover', which will get rid of adhesive labels, tar and chewing gum from china, plastic, fabric and skin as well as glass. It costs £3.95 for 250 ml from Lakeland Plastics; telephone 01539 488100 to order by post. Other solvents that work well are WD40 (wash it off with hot water and washing up liquid as it's rather greasy), white spirit, surgical spirit, acetone or nail varnish remover. Even, I am told, cooking oil does the trick.

Q How should I clean some bone-handled table knives that have yellowed over time?

A This is a bit tricky, as bone handles should never get wet. You should clean your knives after using them by holding the handles and simply wiping down the blades with a cloth. If the handles have ever come into contact with water, the surface will have

Jane Asher's

become flaky, which may explain your current problem. However, repairs are possible. The experts I spoke to in the silver department at Asprey (020 7493 6767) are sure they'll be able to work miracles on your knives.

Q I have some beautiful tiny silver spoons which are just the right size for eating boiled eggs. Unfortunately they have become yolk-stained and I am finding them hard to clean.

A Try rubbing the spoons with salt before washing them in mild detergent.

Q I have a lovely tall, thin-necked crystal decanter . . . with water-marks inside. I have tried removing them with crushed eggshells, very fine sand, Vim, a handy strip of plastic with scouring pad attached, vinegar, lemon juice, Viakal, Harpic, Fairy Liquid and Ariel, and I have even put it in the dishwasher. But nothing works. Please help – it is becoming an obsession.

A My grandmother always taught me to clean the inside of a decanter with lead shot, whirled round and round until all the marks came off. But as that was several decades ago, I thought I ought to check on the latest thinking – so I went straight to the top and asked Asprey. They recommend Steradent (now there's one you didn't think to try!). In their experience, this should get rid of any calcification: just fill the decanter with water, pop in the tablet and leave overnight, then rinse well. Dry the decanter with a hairdryer on a low setting (don't hold it too near the glass) and leave it in the airing cupboard until completely dry. If you reckon your watermarks are due to drips rather than calcification, skip the Steradent and cut to the hairdryer. What would Granny have thought?

Q **My son, a bachelor, recently gave a dinner party that ended rather late so the washing up was left until the next morning. To his dismay, the fish knives (which are marked 'stainless nickel') were stained – they had had mayonnaise and salad dressing on them. Can you suggest a way to remove these marks? The knives are old – a present to me years ago – and have never been used until now.**

A Oh dear, I assume you've tried one of the many stainless steel cleaners you can buy in hardware shops? If they don't work, you could try the secret remedy used by someone who works at a rather smart Regent Street establishment in London. She makes a mild bleach solution and puts the cutlery in that – watching it all the time – until the marks disappear. Rinse everything well afterwards, of course. I have also heard that soaking in biological white washing powder overnight does the trick – I'm all for letting those enzymes do the work for us. But did you know your son was going to use your never-before-eaten-with knives and forks? If not, put him on washing-up duty for six months to atone. I assume he's too old to have his pocket money docked.

Q **I have an antique canteen of silver cutlery that has seen better days. How should I clean it?**

A I would contact the professionals: try Richard Lawton on 020 7404 0487 and Asprey (Top Table Department) on 020 7493 6767.

Q **What can I do about stained china tea cups? Ordinary washing up liquid doesn't seem to get them clean.**

A An overnight soak in Persil (washing powder solution) should work a treat.

Q **A dear old lady has given me quite a large amount of bed linen. Unfortunately, her cupboards must have been quite damp and I can't seem to get rid of the linen's musty smell, even after having washed and ironed it several times.**

A I know just the smell you mean. I have memories of, as a child, staying in country houses where the sheets smelled of a mixture of mushrooms and wet seaweed. Nostalgia apart, I think a night is better spent in fresher surroundings, and I'm glad to say there's a simple answer. Provided the linen is machine washable, Jeeves, launderers and dry cleaners of Belgravia (020 8809 3232) suggest that you make up a special solution in which to pre-soak the linen: for every one gallon of hand-warm water, use one egg cup-full of domestic ammonia and half a tea cup of domestic bleach. Add the chemicals carefully to the water and mix well, then add the linen and soak for an hour. Run the items through the washing machine with your usual detergent and all should be well. If anything is too precious to go in the machine (antique linen and lace need lots of TLC), Lunn Antiques (020 7736 4638) offer a laundry and restoration service for £20 an hour plus VAT. It might be wise to get an estimate first in case they use some special slow, ancient technique.

Q **How can I clean stained and yellowing old pillows? They are filled with curled duck feathers.**

A Most dry-cleaners can re-cover them and refill them with the original (sterilized) feathers. It's not as expensive as it sounds – usually about £8, but well worth it if you'd like to keep everything spick and span.

Q **The ceramic wall tiles inside my shower cubicle have become dull and chalky with the accumulation of splashes. How can I clean them?**

A I would suggest you try Scrub Brite by Armway (01908 363184), or Viakal, which is widely available.

Q I have just moved into a house with a marble fireplace. It looks as if it has not been cleaned for years, but I do not want to use a product that might destroy it. What can you recommend?

A The best course of action is to ring UK Marble on 01432 352178. They should be able to advise you of the best way to clean your hearth.

Q A few months ago we moved into a lovely new house that has UPVC windows and, try as I might, I cannot get the window panes to shine. When the sun shines on them I see nothing but streaks. Have you got any tips? Also, where can I buy T-shirts by Jil Sander?

A What a lovely mix of questions: do the smart ladies in your neighbourhood clean their windows in Jil Sander T-shirts? I understand how important it is to keep up with the Joneses: Harrods is the answer for the shirt. Now, the windows. Of course, the sun is a killer for showing up those missed corners and little streaks, but the Glass and Glazing Federation assures me that UPVC windows should be cleaned just like any other: the technical advisor I spoke to recommends methylated spirits and plenty of elbow grease (I thought it was vinegar and newspaper, but never mind). Dazzle them in your Jil Sander and perhaps the neighbours won't notice the streaks anyway.

Q The white decoration on my green Wedgwood has become discoloured. I have tried gently brushing it with a nail brush in warm soapy water but it doesn't seem to make any difference.

A Experts at Waterford Wedgwood say that a product called Barkeeper's Friend (available from household stores) should do the trick. Can't think why barkeepers in particular need to polish up their Wedgwood, but there you are. It is also effective with porcelain. Alternatively, you could apply some nail polish remover with a soft cloth. If these two solutions don't work, call their customer services line on 01782 282293 and discuss the possibility of sending your pieces back to the factory for analysis.

Q I have some old silver candlesticks. They are so ornate that, when cleaning, I find it almost impossible to clean off all traces of polish. What do you suggest?

A Try using a damp, soft old toothbrush on them to remove the excess polish.

Q The roll of honour for the Second World War in our church is made of brass, the non-polishing kind. Above it lives a family of bats who have made a right old mess all down it. Do you know of anything we could wash it down with?

A Brass cleaning can be tricky, and the best solution is to call in the services of a metal polisher (see your local Yellow Pages for a number) as they'll be able to restore the brasses to their former

Jane Asher's

glory – even, with any luck, the mysterious 'non-polishing' kind. As for the bats, remember that they are a protected species in this country, so it would be well worth calling the Bat Conservation Trust's helpline on 020 7627 8822 for additional advice. They have carried out a three-year study into bats and churches, so are well qualified to suggest various solutions – for example, putting up boarding to stop any future damage. That way, you'll be able to preserve the roll of honour for generations to come as well as looking after the smaller, winged members of your church's congregation. After all, bats in the belfry are only too common, aren't they?

Q Could you help me find a small machine for washing jewellery? Or are they for the trade only?

A I didn't realize how dirty jewellery could get until I had a bracelet mended a few years ago and the jeweller cleaned it before returning it. It was a revelation – it looked like new. You can wash certain items gently in warm soapy water (be careful of gold, as it scratches easily), but a much safer option is to zap them clean with ultrasonic rays in special little machines – I think this may be the sort of thing you have in mind. Contact Sutton Tools on 0121 236 7139; Scientific and Chemical Supplies on 01902 402402, or H S Walsh on 020 8778 7061. They sell small models that can be used at home, but at around £175 each you may not feel it's worth it unless you have lots of jewellery to care for and, in any case, if you have any particularly valuable or fragile items, professional cleaning at a jeweller's is always the best and safest way. Pearls, by the way, should never be cleaned, as the skin's natural oils apparently improve their glossiness, but they can be polished with a chamois just to get the dirt off.

Since writing the above, several readers have written in to tell me that ultrasonic cleaners are available for as little as £20. Ask at your local jewellers for more information. Thank you all for letting me know – none of us need suffer the disgrace of dirty diamonds any longer. Or . . . one reader's mother used to swear that soaking diamond rings in neat gin made them sparkle!

Q We have two sheepskin mats in our bedroom which need a good clean. Can I put them through the washing machine or should I hand wash them?

A I think an ordinary wash would ruin them, and I've been advised that dry cleaning is the only way to clean sheepskin successfully. (How on earth all those sheep out in the fields manage to get themselves to Sketchley's every week is a mystery).

Q I have several books from my late sister's flat that have been stored in a damp cupboard and I cannot rid them of the damp, musty smell. I have kept them in a warm room for several weeks without success. Is there a solution?

The trick is to get some air between the leaves, so keep the books open, which will also stop the pages sticking together, and turn the pages now and then as they are drying. When you eventually put them back into a bookcase, a few drops of lavender oil on the shelves will prevent the mould returning. You don't mention whether the books are bound in leather or cloth, but the chances are that the covers will need some attention, too. Leather can crack if it is not fed, so if your books are leather-bound use something such as hide food (available from saddlers) to nourish it back to health. The waxy, lanolin smell will also help to mask any mustiness. Clean cloth-bound books using a small amount of detergent on some very slightly dampened cotton wool and gently wiping over the surface, stopping at once if any colour comes off. If you need a hand along the way, The Abbey Bookbindery, who supplied the above advice, will help restore anything from Granny's heirloom Bible or a precious 15th-century leather-bound tome to a collection of paperbacks that have seen better days. Call them on 01252 837580 or visit their website at www.bookbinders.co.uk for more information.

Q I recently acquired an oil painting that has been hanging in a pub for the past 30 years. As you can imagine, it's in a bad way due to cigarette smoke and a few beer stains. Is there any way that I can clean it myself without damaging it?

A If I were you I wouldn't go near it with a cloth, or anything else for that matter. One false move and you could find yourself down to the canvas. The Association of Picture Restorers says that every painting has its own quirky problems and could easily be damaged if you're not an expert. Contact them and they'll put you in touch with someone who can help. They are at Station Avenue, Kew, Surrey TW9 3QA, telephone 020 8948 5644. You never know: you might find a Rembrandt under all that smoke.

Q I have a garden table and chairs in white plastic but they have been out in the open all year round and unfortunately the chairs have become very stained and covered in mildew. Is there something that would clean them or could I paint them dark green?

A Yes, mildew on your bottom all summer doesn't sound very appealing. Painting isn't really an option as it would soon crack – plastic simply flexes too much. Instead, I'd suggest a miraculous-sounding product called Nilco UPVC cleaner, which claims to make plastic garden furniture look like new again. A 500-ml bottle costs £2.95 from Lakeland Plastics; telephone 01539 488100 to order.

Q Being a devoted dad, I clean my children's shoes every Sunday night before they go to school and use the traditional wax polish and brushes as it gives the best results. It takes a while, though, so my wife has suggested that I use one of those instant-shine sponge applicators instead – the kids could even help as it's so easy. I think they're awful, but should I sacrifice old-fashioned standards for convenience?

A I have to declare a nostalgic prejudice – I have clear childhood memories of my father cleaning my shoes in the old-fashioned way just as you do, and I can still smell the polish and see the deep rich shine that it put on them. But I must admit that, in spite of my father's example, I'm very bad at doing my own shoes and I always used one of the instant applicators on my children's: they are remarkably quick and efficient and cover all the scuffs. How about doing them your way every couple of weeks to feed the leather and touching up in between with the cheat's method?

Q During a moment of carelessness while eating a cream tea, a small splash of cream fell onto a suede jacket that I was wearing. I tried to sponge it off with a mild detergent, to no avail. It has now dried, but the small stain is still there.

A Suede has a mysterious habit of eating up most stains. I have some beautiful suede trousers that a dry cleaning specialist advised me to leave well alone when I spilt food on them, and the marks eventually disappeared, but in your case they tell me that talc may be the answer. Dust a little onto the grease spot and leave for a while. The powder should absorb the oil and can then simply be brushed off, leaving (with luck) completely stain-free suede underneath.

Q **I attended a party recently and the host was sticking an ornament with super glue. When he shook my hand a small spot of the glue was deposited on the cuff on my blazer. Could you kindly advise me if there is a method by which it could be removed? I have tried nail polish remover without success.**

A As I read your letter I thought you were going to tell us that you and your host were still joined together hand to hand – the cuff was a bit of a let down. It's bad news getting this sort of glue on fabric as it bonds the fibres together pretty comprehensively, but there are a couple of things you could try. One is warm soapy water, though the chances are your blazer is dry clean only. If that's the case, a special de-bonding solvent (made by the same people as the glue, so you'll have to check with your host) is often recommended. This should soften the glue – wash (the hotter the better) or dry clean it while it's still soft, and that should do the trick.

Q **How can I clean a fake fur leopard skin coat? If possible I'd like to get it done by post as I do not have a car.**

A There are a couple of companies who offer cleaning services by post: Gale Furs, 65 Regents Park Road, London NW1, telephone 020 7722 5870; and Noble Furs, 3 New Burlington Place,

London W1, telephone 020 7734 6394.

Q **My grandson plays rugby and, try as I might, I can't get his rugby shirts clean.**

A My sons play rugby and I have exactly the same problems. I have found it just isn't possible to get them as white as those TV commercials would have us believe. I soak them overnight in detergent, then the next morning scrub the mud off and wash them on a cycle of 50 degrees. But even after all that I don't get total success. It's probably because rugby players spend almost the entire match rolling around in the mud, whereas footballers tend to stay on their feet a little more. For grass stains you could try saturating the area with white spirit, then rinse and wash.

DYEING

Q **I am looking for someone who will dye my wedding dress for me. It's a lovely style and is designer-made, so it seems a shame not to be able to wear it more than just the once.**

A Dyeing a wedding dress seems to be fraught with problems, and there's only one company in the country that will still take it on – Giltbrook Dyers and Cleaners in Nottingham. The first consideration is the material – only natural fabrics are suitable. Even if the main body of your dress is silk or cotton, the lace trim and even the thread may be synthetic and will absorb the dye differently. Second, there are risks involved in the dyeing process which mean that there's a strong possibility that your dress may shrink, tear or split at the seams. Third, it's not cheap: prices start at around £71.50. Last of all, the range of colours is limited to just six shades, unless you want to pay even more. If, after all that, you still decide to go ahead, call 0115 938 2231 for a special mail order pack. But I wonder if you might regret it? Memories are so precious that you might be better off keeping the dress as it is – I always think dyeing changes the feel of a fabric. For the cost involved in dyeing, you might find a local dress-maker to copy the original style in a cheaper fabric, or perhaps alter the length and style so that it's wearable in its existing white or cream.

Jane Asher's

Q While bleaching some laundry I splashed a favourite cashmere jumper. What can I do?

A I'm afraid it is impossible to remove bleach stains, but it might be worth you speaking to your local dry cleaners who will probably have some advice as to whether it would be possible to dye your jumper successfully.

Q I thought I might give my wardrobe a bit of a lift this summer by dyeing some boring pale-coloured T-shirts and trousers in bright colours. I love vibrant pinks and lilacs and thought this would fit in with this season's floaty feminine styles. The last thing I dyed was a disastrous tie-dye scarf in the seventies, so I am slightly scared to embark on this new venture. I know that you can now buy dyes that go in the washing machine, but am terrified that this will make all my washing pink for ever more. Any idea how to do it properly?

A Tie-dying is second only to macramé on my list of time-wasting crafts that produce unattractive results, so I'm pleased you're now opting for the one-colour look. Dying clothes is extremely easy these days, as sticking them in the washing machine means you won't get dye where you don't want it and won't end up with blotches and streaks of colour by accident. And the colour really does miraculously disappear from the machine afterwards so you won't end up with pink knickers – I promise. Dylon Machine Dyes cost round £4.45 and come in plenty of colours, including some pretty summery pinks, violets and blues, and will dye up to 1 lb (dry weight) of clothes made from cotton, linen or viscose. You'll get lighter shades if you use it on polyester/cotton mixes, as synthetics don't pick up the dye as well as natural fabrics. For any questions, including how to dye dark colours light using a special Pre-Dye, call Dylon's consumer advice line on 020 8663 4296. If you're interested, they can even tell you where you went wrong with that tie-dying all those years ago (apart, of course, from deciding to do it in the first place).

I have a red leather jacket that I would like to dye black. Do you know of a company who will do this for me?

I'm afraid not – the only companies I know of dye other fabrics, or dye only bags and shoes. Maybe you should sell it and buy another with the proceeds?

Jane Asher's

CARING FOR FABRICS

Q Can you tell me how to store a silk smocked, embroidered, beaded, long christening gown worn recently by our six-month-old daughter? It is unlikely to be required again until she has children of her own. It has been successfully dry cleaned, but where can I get materials to keep it safe for the future? Mail order would be ideal.

A The Textile Restoration Studio has the answer. The crucial points are to use acid-free materials and no folding (silk is so delicate that a fold can eventually make the fibres split). The trick is to form con-certinaed rolls of acid-free tissue paper and put them between the layers of fabric so that any folds become gently curved, packing out the bodice and sleeves with more paper. Keep the whole thing in a box that is also acid-free, has reinforced corners and is durable enough for long-term storage. The studio supplies all these materials in a kit – the one for a christening gown includes a 20- x 16- x 3-inch acid-free box, 20 sheets of acid-free tissue paper and full instructions. It costs £25 and can be ordered by post from 2 Talbot Road, Bowdon, Altrincham, Cheshire, WA14 3JD, telephone 0161 928 0020, or send an A4 SAE for a brochure. Larger sizes are available for wedding dresses and other precious items of clothing. The studio suggests putting other things associated with the christening or wedding inside the box, making sure that only acid-free paper comes into contact with the gown, of course.

Q I am nervous about trusting my wedding dress to a local dry cleaner, but I know that if I don't get it cleaned the fabric will yellow and any stains will worsen.

A You are right to want to clean it properly. Call the Fabric Care and Research Association on 01423 885977 who will recommend a good dry cleaner in your area for wedding dresses and other special outfits.

Q How can I stop my chenille jumpers from shedding?

A It's infuriating isn't it? You've only got to take your favourite cardy from the drawer and suddenly the house is under a layer of fluff. Textile technologists tell me that it's a feature of this type of yarn that the fibres are held in place fairly loosely – in other words, chenille will always shed bits. So much for those men in white coats! The best advice is to handle it gently and to avoid using fabric softeners, which reduce friction so the fibres slip apart.

Q Please can you tell me the secret of keeping pure silk blouses soft? I buy them because I love the almost suede-like feel of them – until they are washed, that is. I have tried all sorts of things to no avail. My shirts still end up board-hard, which is very disappointing. Please can you help me before I give up buying them altogether?

Jane Asher's

A I've had the same trouble, so I asked silk specialists Tie Rack, who sell everything from silk blouses to scarves as well as ties. Silk is surprisingly easy to care for with simple washing and drying – but you do have to be gentle with it as it is extremely delicate. First, always hand-wash your shirts inside out (who'd have thought it?) and use a mild liquid soap solution that is specially formulated for silk; never ordinary biological or non-biological detergents. Don't leave your blouses to soak, and never wring or twist them to get rid of excess water; squeezing gently should be enough. Don't hang them to dry – put them flat, or, in the case of crêpe de chine, for example, you can tumble dry on cool, which should actually enhance its fluffy surface texture. Use a very cool iron. Do all this and your shirts should stay soft for a lifetime.

Q **I am a busy mum and, what with full-time work and four children to look after, don't usually get round to ironing much of the family laundry, let alone things like sheets and pillowcases (all in cotton, as we hate synthetics). I tend to let body heat work its magic on T-shirts and the like. My great aunt – the most house-proud person on earth – is due to descend on us for a week in the summer holidays. I usually go out of my way to get everything ship-shape for her arrival, but this time I am planning to strike a blow for busy families everywhere and make up her bed with some clean but un-ironed linen. What should I say if there's any sniping about slipping standards?**

A I'm entirely on your side – ironing sheets is time-consuming and exhausting, but I know it can be hard for older people to understand. How about laughing merrily if she mentions the creased bed and explaining that these are the very latest trendily textured sheets? Rather like scrunch-dried hair, they are of course meant to look unkempt but in fact take hours of work to arrange in those little wrinkles . . . Or – more seriously – how about explaining to her that you usually prepare her room as you would for a visiting guest, but this time felt close enough to her to treat her as one of the family? Sit beside her on the un-ironed bed and chat woman to woman about the demands of home, children and so on and she may well begin to understand just what it's like for you. Or, if you want to avoid any possibility of sniping, why not invest in a set of Marks & Spencer's new range of non-iron cotton bed linen?

Q **I want to rearrange the furniture in my living room for a party, but I know that when I move the chairs, sofa and coffee table there will be heavy indentations in the carpet. Do I just have to wait for the carpet to get itself back to normal or is there a way of speeding up the process?**

A You would have to wait several weeks for the carpet to regain its flat surface, but I have found that a good trick for removing these tell-tale dents quickly is to apply moisture from a steam iron and brush until the nap rises. Rubbing the dents with an ice-cube can also work wonders. Or you could invite so many people to your party that no one notices the carpet.

REPAIRS

Q I have a porcelain American Eagle but recently, while dusting, I managed to knock it over. Do you know where I could get it professionally repaired? Or could I tackle the job myself?

A The company China Repairers have frequently come to the rescue of over-enthusiastic dusters. Call them on 020 8444 3030, and arrange to take your piece along. They can do two levels of repair, either of which will be far better than anything you might achieve with a tube of glue at home: museum standard, which involves sticking, filling and touching up the damage and starts at £15, or an invisible repair, which includes additional airbrushing over the break to get rid of any signs of damage and costs from £35. The former sounds pretty good to me – the idea of anything in the house being of 'museum standard' sounds very impressive.

Q I have a glass candlestick, the stem of which has broken off its base after encountering my granddaughter. It is one of a pair that were a wedding present to my mother in 1921, so I would dearly love to have it repaired.

A This reminds me horribly of when our daughter, aged two, neatly snapped the head off an extremely valuable Minoan figure which belonged to someone we'd only just met. The figure was at perfect toddler height on a coffee table . . . I'm glad to tell you that your candlestick will be considerably easier to mend and at a very reasonable cost. The expert restorers at Wilkinsons say that, provided the two sections marry up well, it's a fairly straightforward job and should cost around £10 plus VAT. The repairs are almost invisible – all you should see afterwards is a slight crack. It can all be done by post (well-padded and registered). Call 020 8314 1080 for details.

Q **When I washed my chintz curtains the glaze came off. What can I do to restore it?**

A I don't know of a product you can use at home, but Cadogan Company (020 8960 8020) will be able to help you – they are a chintz re-glazing specialist.

Q **How do you cure a creaky bed? My husband and I have a rather ancient divan that squeaks really badly – just turning over is enough to wake the neighbours, let alone anything else. I'd love to know if there's a remedy.**

A The words 'rather ancient' say it all, I'm afraid. If it was a new bed, I'd recommend taking it straight back to the shop and complaining like mad, but because it's a bit long in the tooth, that's not really an option. According to The Sleep Council, a divan bed or mattress has a natural lifespan of only around 8 or 10 years. After that, squeaking can be caused by anything from rusty springs to loosening of the bed's structure. Whichever it is, there isn't really a cure, apart from shelling out for a new bed, which

Jane Asher's

will surely be a priority as it must be inhibiting both your sleep and your love life.

 I have a set of bone-handled cutlery. The bone is so worn that I'd like to look into the possibility of replacing it with metal. How should I go about this?

 I would ask the Top Table department at Asprey's for advice. They are at 165–169 New Bond Street, London W1, telephone 020 7493 6767.

 The zip on my suitcase is broken. Can I mend or replace it?

 Mending a zip sounds easy, but in this case would in fact be so expensive that you may as well buy a new suitcase – I'm afraid this is one of the perils of mass production.

 One of the burners on my Tricity Moffat cooker has stopped working. What should I do?

The best thing to do would be to call Customer Services at Tricity Moffat for advice. They are generally extremely helpful and their telephone number is 0990 805805.

Q I have an old Hoover washing machine that is playing up. Should I chuck it out and start again, or can I get it reconditioned?

A It's possible that you might find a local reconditioning company who can help, but it might be better to call Hoover direct on 01685 721222 and ask their advice.

Q The dark green wooden window sills on the outside of my house seem to be cracking. Can I just repaint or should I replace them altogether?

A It depends on the condition of the wood. If it is unsound you will have to replace the sills. If not, call the British Decorator's Association on 024 7635 3776 and they will help you find someone locally to advise. Painting them in a light colour in the future will help to prevent cracking as it reflects the heat better. It's the heat which causes damage as it makes air pockets in badly prepared surfaces which expand, thereby causing cracks and allowing in more water.

Q My black leather coat is fading and drying out in places. What can I do to save it?

A The best advice I can offer is to buy a leather nourisher – try shoe shops or dry cleaners to find it.

Q How can I adjust the bands inside hats to make them fit my small head?

A I have the opposite problem, and most hats are too tight on me. There are two ways of getting yours to fit: either the proper milliner's solution or an easier cheat's method. The first involves taking small tucks in the petersham ribbon inside the hat. Start about an inch away from the mid-point at the back and take in a small pleat, stitching it to hold. Then do the same at the other side and try it for size; if it's still too big, repeat the process further round the band as necessary. The second, more modern, way is to put draught excluder (handy if it's a bit windy on the day) or self-adhesive Velcro strip under the petersham ribbon to pack it out and make the hat fit more closely. If you're using Velcro, buy the type that comes in inch-wide strips and use one half of it at a time cut to the correct length until you get the desired fit. It's worth adding a few stitches here and there just to keep it all in place – if the wind blows you won't be left standing there wearing nothing but a rather quirky headband.

REDECORATING

Q When we converted our house 10 years ago, we put in a reproduction pine fireplace surround. I have now gone off it, particularly as it is discoloured with a yellowish tinge and looks wrong with the mahogany furniture in the room. Can we paint it? (The room is turquoise.) I can't afford to take the fireplace out.

A The yellowish tinge with your turquoise walls doesn't sound very attractive, I must say. But don't despair, there are many ways to bring your pine back to life. Liming it would be a quick solution – it would give the wood a brighter, sun-bleached look. But if your heart is set on painting it to link in with your turquoise scheme then a woodwash would give a more subtle effect than a coat of gloss. There are plenty of ideas and hints on preparing the surface in *Country Living*'s inspirational *Paint Recipe Book* by Liz Wagstaff (Quadrille, £9.99).

Q I have just spent a fortune having my roof replaced, which means that I can finally decorate over all the watermarks on my ceilings that have been there since the rain came through last winter. I have tried sloshing some white emulsion over the top, but the pale brown tinge still comes through. Do I have to paint my whole flat beige to disguise them?

A No, you don't, luckily (the colour 'watermark beige' doesn't sound too chic, does it?). All you have to do is use a special primer under the emulsion to stop the stains showing through. If there's any mould or mildew, remove that first with a proprietary cleaner, then leave to dry thoroughly. Buy something such as Dulux Alkali Resisting Primer or International's Universal Primer Sealer (both cost around £8 for 1 litre) and, with the room well ventilated, use it to cover the watermarks. Then you can decorate over the top with emulsion in any colour under the sun without worrying about the brown re-emerging. Don't forget to stop the rain getting in again, though, or you'll be back where you started.

Q My son and daughter-in-law have just moved into an old Victorian house which needs quite a bit of redecoration – it seems years since it had a new coat of paint. My daughter-in-law is very worried about stripping off the old paint work in case it is lead-based, especially as she has a baby and a three-year-old. What is the best way to deal with it?

A She is right to be cautious as lead-based paints are harmful to health, especially where young children and pregnant women are concerned. Lead was used widely as a pigment in white paint until the 1950s; after that its use was controlled and now it is longer permitted in household paints in the UK. If you suspect your home may be affected, the first step is to check out the situation for sure – this can be done with a special testing kit, available from stores such as B & Q for less than £3. The chemical components turn red when they come into contact with lead in a painted surface. If your suspicions are confirmed, there are various things to bear in mind if you are planning to remove it. First, don't use a blow lamp or gas torch to burn the paint off as this will release dangerous fumes; hot air guns or chemical strippers are preferable. Second, don't use dry sandpaper as this will fill the house with lead-rich dust; use wet-and-dry instead. Third, don't use an ordinary vacuum cleaner to clear up afterwards as the filters are unlikely to be fine enough to retain the lead dust; hire an efficient industrial vacuum cleaner with heavy-duty filters. If a lot of work needs to be done, or if the paint work is flaking badly, it would be wise to get a professional in to tackle the job for you – it really is best to err on the side of caution here.

Q We have just moved into an old house with ceilings that have Artex in between the beams. The idea is to restore the rooms in period style, so we need somehow to give the plaster a smooth finish again. Artex seems like devilishly hard stuff to shift – is there a secret?

A The chances are you'll be dealing with one of two kinds of textured finish. The first is really easy to get off – all you do is load a sponge with soapy water and apply it to the surface, which then dissolves into a paste that can simply be scraped off. The second is a waterproof variety, so you'll need to use a special textured paint remover to get rid of it – try one made by Nitromors, available from hardware stores and builders' merchants. But a

Jane Asher's

simpler solution involves a bit of lateral thinking: instead of removing it why not add to it? You can change the texture by applying a layer of Artex skim coat to smooth out the lumps and bumps. This is available from B & Q (costing around £9.99 for a 10-kg bag) and gives you a surface that is ready to be covered with paint, wallpaper or whatever.

Since writing this, a reader has written in to chide me that this method can be very messy, and suggests the far cheaper alternative of using liquid bonding applied with a brush, then a coat of Thistle finishing plaster (approximately £5 for 25 kg). I'd suggest you get a good plasterer to do it as it's not really a job for DIY.

Q **My son and his partner have recently moved house and the brick fireplace is covered in white paint. Is there any way they can remove it so the natural brickwork is exposed again?**

A There's a product called Peelaway which can strip up to 30 layers of paint in one go. (Do be careful, though – presumably it would make very light work of your seven or so layers of skin). You apply the paste to the area you need to strip, place a sheet (supplied with the paste) on top, then leave it for a few hours. Peel off the sheet and, hey presto, the paint comes off too. A 3-litre tub costs £12.87 and is available from Layland SDM. For stockists and mail order call 0800 454484.

Q I have a 1-foot-long, white-painted shelf that holds all the medicines and shampoos in my bathroom. How can I make it look more attractive?

A What can't you do with a plain white bathroom shelf? Think of it as a blank canvas, just waiting to be decorated with anything from seashells collected from a beach to one of a thousand paint effects. Have a look in Catrin Cargill's book *Contemporary Painted Furniture* (Ryland Peters & Small, £16.99). Any one of the finishes she describes – from woodgraining and candy stripes to stencils and crackle-glaze – would transform your plain shelf into something wonderful.

Q I am installing a new kitchen and my husband and I disagree about work tops. He says granite ones are best and I want wood, which is much warmer and more user-friendly. Which would you recommend?

A I have a mixture of both in my kitchen. I was initially worried about the coldness and noise of a hard granite surface (and about breaking things) so put it only around the sink, with wood elsewhere. I now wish I'd had granite everywhere: it's much easier to look after and isn't cold and noisy at all; you can put boiling hot pans and tins straight onto it, chop on it, make pastry on it . . . I could go on. And it's so beautiful that I find myself gazing into its depths, thinking about the millennia that have gone into its making. As you can see, I'm a bit besotted. It's expensive, but if you can afford it I'd go for granite – you won't regret it. Mine was supplied by UK Marble. Call them on 01432 352178 for any granite or marble enquiries relating to kitchens or bathrooms.

Q **I am moving house and want the decor as simple as possible. I'd love to paint the walls white but am bamboozled because it now seems to come in a million different shades. How do I know which one to use?**

A It is quite bizarre that we not only have a vast choice of colours in paint nowadays but that even using something as basic as white is fraught with indecision. On the whole, I can't help thinking that any old white would do, but after talking to the experts I can see they have a point. Brilliant white is the easy option and looks stunning in Mediterranean sun; but in darker climes, and especially in artificial light, it can have a harsh, almost bluey tinge. More sympathetic are whites with a touch of warmer pigments in the mix. They tell me Crown's Gull White is many an interior decorator's trade secret.

Q **Our sitting room looks directly onto a busy pavement of people peering in to see what we are doing. Net curtains are naff. Have you any groovier suggestions?**

A I assume you don't want anything that cuts out too much light, so what about muslin? There's nothing naff about it – quite the reverse, in fact, if you check out the houses of those in the know. Another advantage is that it's so cheap (from only £1.85 per metre from Ian Mankin Direct, telephone 020 7722 0997. It is also cheap at John Lewis – 020 7629 7711). This means you can drape yards of it around the window and curtain pole in folds and swags. I know that can be easier said than done – some people seem to be natural drapers and swaggers and some don't, and I'm not – but keep trying until it looks right. Alternatively, if your budget will stretch to it, why not fit shutters? Either half-shutters or split ones with a top section that can be folded back would give you back your privacy. Look for designs with louvred panels that can be moved to let in more light without allowing passers by to peek. Made-to-measure solutions are available from The Shutter Shop, telephone 01252 844575.

Q I am looking for some specific wall tiles to match a design on the tiles in my bathroom. Where should I start my search?

A It is worth getting in touch with the Reject Tile Shop, 178 Wandsworth Bridge Road, London SW6, telephone 020 7731 6098.

Q I've just moved out of London and into a little cottage in Yorkshire – the rural life I've always dreamed of. I'd like a traditional farmhouse kitchen, but don't want to go down the clichéd chintz-and-china route because I'm only 28 and don't want to be old before my time. How can I get the room to look countrified without being too fussy and fuddy-duddy?

Jane Asher's

A I should probably be asking you, as I'm well into the fuddy-duddy age group and fighting the temptation to curl up in a chintz armchair in a cardy with my copy of Saga, but I think you're right – the floral look isn't really on for bright young things such as yourself. I take it that you want something clean and simple that's not too high-tech and clinical-looking. How about a Shaker-style kitchen? I think they look stunning – clean lines, natural materials and no frills. There's plenty of inspiration from Catrin Cargill in *Pure Country* (Ryland Peters and Small, £18.99) – a lovely book that will look good casually left on a coffee table by the inglenook.

Q **We have a granny flat in the basement of our house which has been empty for some time. There is a slightly funny smell down there, and I wonder if it might be damp. Is there a quick way of testing for damp, before having to call in the professionals?**

A Yes there is. If you suspect a room is damp, tape a square piece of aluminium foil over a section of the wall and leave for a day or two. Peel away the foil and check for water droplets underneath. It reminds me of the time my father put a piece of Sellotape over a crack in the wall of the hospital where he worked to check on whether it was still widening. A nurse the next day gently told him she didn't think it would be strong enough to hold the wall together.

RENOVATING AND RESTORING

Q I am moving into an old house with black-painted floor-boards – interestingly gothic but very gloomy, and making everywhere look smaller. We can't afford to carpet, so what else can we do?

A Don't despair! I've spoken to some experts and have some ingenious solutions from *Good Living* and *Change That* interior decorator Lee Jackson. First, try to establish whether the black surface is paint or a wood stain. Scrape a small section of the surface to see what comes off – a layer of paint or the wood itself. If it is the wood itself, it will have been stained, and this is relatively good news as the colour won't have penetrated very deep and can be removed by scrubbing with generous dollops of Nitromors. Finish with a good scrub with white spirit to remove all trace of the stripper. Any gaps between the boards can be filled with special fillets that are triangular in section and can simply be hammered in until flush with the surface. The floor can then be re-stained in a pale shade of teak or rosewood. If, on the other hand, the black stuff was paint, it's not the end of the world: sand it down with a professional sanding machine, then stain or wax in your preferred colour.

Jane Asher's

Q I have decided to decorate a bedroom that hasn't been used for many years. The only problem is that the walls are covered with woodchip paper which has been painted in a very hard emulsion. I have sought professional help and it appears that the only way to remove it would be to steam it off, a long and tedious job. Any alternatives?

A Unfortunately there doesn't seem to be any easy answer. Even professional decorators talk despairingly of this kind of paper: the chips stop the scraper moving smoothly, apparently, which is why it takes so long to get off and why steaming is indeed the best way. I have two suggestions for speeding up the process. One is to insert the point of a sharp knife between the two layers while the paper is still dry, and gradually remove the top one. The under-layer can then be wetted and scraped off in the usual way. The other idea is to use a little hand-held gadget available from DIY shops that scores the paint and allows the steam to penetrate more easily into the paper – this will speed you along a little.

Q I have several items of high-street furniture which have become scratched in places as the surface varnish has peeled. Professionals inform me that my furniture cannot be stripped as it is veneered. Can you advise me please on how to improve its appearance?

A I would consult a French polisher, whose numbers you will find in the Yellow Pages. Much of their work involves stripping and re-polishing veneered furniture. On the other hand, B & Q's advice for DIY enthusiasts is to paint it, perhaps even recreating something of its former glory by finishing it off with a special wood-grain paint effect. A good product to start with is called Easy Surface Prep (available from DIY stores). A coat of ESP, as it's known in the trade, allows paint to stick to any shiny surface such as veneer which would otherwise be unpaintable. Once done, you can use any paints you fancy. Whatever you do, leave time for the surface to cure; it may feel dry but if you used a water-based paint, it will be fragile for anything up to 30 days (one to two weeks for oil-based).

Q I have an old teak Indonesian rice box that we use as a coffee table. Unfortunately it has become marked badly from wet glasses, as coasters do not sit happily on the rough surface. Wood polish doesn't seem to do the trick.

A With unvarnished wood, such as teak, simply rub some mayonnaise into the marks – they will disappear as if by magic. (And make yourself a tuna sandwich while you're at it: although I'm a lover of homemade mayonnaise, there are certain recipes when you just have to use the bought kind for that authentic American taste, and tuna and mayo is one of them.)

Q I have a large oval mahogany table that has unfortunately suffered two scratches. I got in touch with a local furniture restorer who says that the whole table will have to be stripped and re-polished. It was restored about 16 years ago and the work

Jane Asher's

cost over £100 then. As I am now a pensioner, there's no way I can afford to spend that sort of money. Is there a product I could buy so I can just have a go myself?

A Unless the scratches are very deep I think I can recommend just the thing – Liberon Retouch Crayons. All you do is crayon over the scratches, buff the surface to a shine and then wax polish your table as usual, just to blend it all in further. There's a mahogany set, costing £2.99 from hardware shops, which contains three coloured sticks that you either use separately or blend together to match the colour of your table.

Q How should I look after my maple table?

A Maple, teak and mahogany need special care. Rub along the grain with teak or linseed oil about twice a year.

Q A hot casserole was inadvertently placed on my dining room table. What can I do about the burn marks?

A I think the only real solution is to contact a good local furniture restorer. If you check in your Yellow Pages under Furniture Repairs and Restoration you will probably find several suitable companies.

Q I have a set of stainless steel dining chairs with cane seats, but the cane seems to have become brittle and is starting to crack. I know a little about caning but feel that these are constructed with a whole section of cane rather than just individual strands. I wonder if you could help.

A You're right: many pieces of modern cane furniture are made with pre-woven sheets of cane which can easily be replaced. If your chairs have grooves running round the edges of the seats this is certainly the case, but if you see rows of little holes, then the seat needs to be woven from scratch by passing the strands in and out of each hole. Materials for both methods are available by post from The Cane Store, (020 7354 4210) and all you need do is to soak a length of the sheeting in hot water for 40 minutes, which stretches the cane and makes it softer and easier to fit, then hammer it into the grooves, fix with wood glue and fit a length of round cane on top to fill the rest of the groove. Trim off any excess and that's that. They make it sound so easy – I have a feeling I'd end up covered in wood glue and with sheets of cane popping out of my grooves, but maybe unlike me you're a natural chair re-seater. The sheet cane costs £3.15 per linear foot; the round cane is 30p per metre (both prices exclude p & p).

Q I have acquired an old, rather dirty chair with lovely cane bergere work on the back and armrests. It obviously needs re-upholstering but I would like to clean and preserve the bergere work. Should

this be done before or after the upholstery work and what would you suggest I use? The cane feels quite dry.

What a lucky old chair to have found such a good home. The British Antique and Furniture Restorers Association recommend an extremely easy way to perk up the cane bits. You may be pleased to know that you should not attempt to re-cane it: that would automatically devalue it. Dry, brittle canes are a common problem and all you have to do is apply a few coats of raw linseed oil with a brush, probably from the back as it may not soak in through the glaze on the front. Leave the last coat to soak in for about a week. It may change the colour of the cane but this should improve as it dries out, and the process will certainly restore its flexibility. If you'd like to consult an expert first, call BAFRA on 01305 854822 for a member in your area.

Is it possible to repaint a Lloyd Loom chair? I would like to strip and respray one that has previously been hand-painted. Is this a pipe dream?

In your case, I'm afraid I may have bad news: Lloyd Loom furniture is always spray-painted in the factory, and it's only possible to respray items that have seen better days provided this finish hasn't been tampered with. It's just a question of cleaning and preparing the fibres properly before spraying on a new coat. Although I have heard of some people who have had success using car spray, the people at Lloyd Loom tell me you can't strip the furniture – so if some helpful person has previously painted your chair using a brush, which from the sound of it is what happened to yours, then they will have clogged up the fibres and, sadly, your chair is probably beyond redemption. To make doubly sure, before you relegate your chair to a dark corner do check with the makers themselves: Lloyd Loom of Spalding produce a special free factsheet on restoring and repainting their furniture. For a copy, send an SAE to them at Wardentree Lane, Pinchbeck, Spalding, Lincs PE11 3SY. If you need to patch up any frayed yarn or braiding, there is also a special Lloyd Loom repair kit – call 01775 712111 for details.

Q **I have a leather-topped table that has seen better days. Can you recommend some professional restorers?**

A Try contacting Antique Leathers (Wincanton) on 01963 33163, Brighton Regency Leathers on 01273 557418, or Leather Conservation Centre (Northampton) 01604 719766.

Q **Is it possible to dye a multicoloured stair carpet dark brown? It's a ghastly combination of beige, brown and apricot, but it's expensive Axminster so I'm loath to part with it.**

A The National Institute of Carpet and Floorlayers is very definite on this: don't attempt it under any circumstances. But as it's an expensive carpet and in good condition, why don't you sell it? An auction house would probably be the best bet, or an ad in a newspaper or magazine. Alternatively, you can try to love it. Does it help at all if you think of it as kitsch rather than hideous?

Q We have a problem in our church. Some time ago it was necessary to lift part of the floor to have some pipework replaced. When it came to refitting the wood blocks, no one could remember how they were originally laid. We also need to replace a number of other blocks, which we are advised are pitch pine, but despite all our efforts we have not been able to find a supplier.

A I have a wonderful image of you all standing around trying to replace the blocks like pieces in a jigsaw. I have spoken to a company who say it is '100 per cent sure' that it will be able to supply the wood you're after. It is called Victorian Wood Works, and it holds £4 million-worth of old timber in stock for precisely this kind of job. They have a team of fitters who'll be able to tell you how to put your floor back together again. Call 020 8534 1000 to discuss your requirements. There is also an amazing company called Salvo, a mine of information on anything to do with architectural salvage. For £5.75 it will send out a pack that includes a list of reputable dealers in each area. It is a great source of information for anyone undertaking restoration work or with a passion for old buildings. Call 01890 820333 for more information.

Q I have a black Cornish slate fire hearth which, unfortunately, has become marked by cup and glass rings over the years. How do I restore it to its former glory?

A The wine must flow pretty freely in your house if your friends end up lying on the floor with their glasses in the grate. Maybe a coffee table would be a good investment? Meanwhile, assuming your hearth is smooth, finished slate – as opposed to the rough, riven sort – then the following, courtesy of Alfred McAlpine Slate in North Wales, should do the trick. Use the very finest grade of wet and dry emery paper (600 or 800 grit) with a bit of water and rub over the surface to remove any marks and scratches. Then darken the slate again with either a specialist slate sealant or a mixture of boiled linseed oil and white spirit. The other option is a wonderful farmhouse remedy: rub on some full cream milk with a soft cloth, let it dry, then buff up with another soft cloth. I am assured it won't smell, and even if it does, maybe it'll keep your guests upright for a change.

Q The surface of my taps has become worn. Where can I get them re-plated?

A There are several companies who re-plate taps: The Bath Doctor (Kent) on 01233 740532, Bathshield (East Sussex) on 01342 823243, and Stiffkey Bathrooms (Norfolk) on 01328 830099.

Jane Asher's

Q I have just moved into an old house which I am trying to renovate. Some of the taps are encrusted with hard water deposits, and I don't want to attempt to chip them off in case I damage the taps. Can you recommend a product for dealing with this problem?

A Limescale-removing products should work, but a simple but useful technique is to fill a plastic sandwich bag with dissolved water softener or vinegar and tie onto the tap. Leave it for 2 hours and the hard deposits should come away easily.

Q We have been renting out the basement of our house for the past year and it is now empty again. The grouting between the bathroom tiles has gone mouldy and black – what should I do to restore them to their former glory?

A Try cleaning them with an old toothbrush dipped in a solution of half bleach, half water. Make sure the bleach doesn't touch the bath or basin as it will damage the enamel. If this doesn't work, you may have to consider re-grouting.

Q I have a Chinese rug, one end of which is fraying. I would like to try to repair it myself, but do not know where to get hold of the materials.

A Textile Restoration Studios supply a mail order catalogue of materials needed for textile conservation. Their telephone number is 0161 928 0020.

Q I have just bought an old enamel bread bin from a junk shop – the kind with 'Bread' written on it, just in case I ever forget what I should use it for. It's quite old and so has obviously seen better days. Can I touch up the odd chip and scratch with enamel paint or is there any other way to give it a bit of a face lift?

A The experts at Kitchen Bygones, who stock all sorts of old equipment at their shop in Alfie's Antique Market, 13–25 Church Street, London NW8, say that touching up with enamel paint is not really an option, as this not only devalues the item but also usually ends up looking a bit second-rate as colour-matching the paint is so difficult. The chips and scratches you describe are inherent to the charm of these pieces, so the best thing is to keep them there. (This has to be the best excuse for not bothering to repair things that I've ever heard – I shall be using it frequently.) Remove any rust on the outside with an abrasive metal polish from a car body shop, then buff up the cast iron that is revealed underneath with black grate polish, available from hardware stores. This should prevent further rusting. Don't try this on old enamel saucepans or plates, though, as the health and hygiene risks are all too obvious; if these are damaged, it's time to use them as decorative plant pots I'm afraid.

Q My husband and I went away on a romantic weekend to celebrate my birthday and we stayed in a lovely hotel – complete with four-poster, breakfast in bed and indulgent piles of fluffy towels. Why do hotel towels always seem so soft and luxurious while the ones at home come off the line like cardboard?

Jane Asher's

A I love staying in hotels but as I live in London I never normally use them here. However, when I was presenting some awards at the Dorchester last year, I was lent a suite to change in and the towels were the fluffiest and softest I've ever felt, so when I got your letter I knew exactly whom to ask. The head housekeeper at the Dorchester says that first you've got to buy the right sort of towels: only the very best heavy Egyptian or Turkish cotton will do. Always wash them at the correct recommended temperature; don't use a lot of fabric conditioner as it can reduce absorbency, and don't use bleach as it can rot the fibres. Steeping towels overnight in mild detergent is far more effective. The drying stage is critical – don't let your towels get too hot and never dry them on a source of direct heat, which is the quickest way to turn them into sandpaper. Don't press them either (good news); just shake and fold and hey presto, fluffy bathtime bliss.

Q **A hairline crack has appeared on a favourite earthenware jug and it is no longer watertight. I use it a lot for flowers and wonder if there is something that would seal it again and stop it leaking.**

A I have exactly the same problem but have never bothered to find out what to do about it, so we'll be trying this together. According to a potter friend, hairline cracks like the ones you describe are inherent in country pottery because the glaze often shrinks more than the body of the pot when it cools down after firing, putting it under tension and making it craze into small cracks. Country pottery is also often fired at low temperatures, which means that the clay does not vitrify and remains porous. Together, these two factors make for pots that aren't entirely watertight – as we have discovered. But there is a clever trick that should solve the problem without altering the vase's appearance. First, put the vase somewhere warm (the airing cupboard is ideal) for a week or so to make sure that the body of the pot is bone dry. Then pour a small tin of yachting varnish into the vase. Pour it back into the tin, turning the pot as you go so that the inside is evenly coated. Stand the pot upside-down on a rack to dry, then paint the bottom with varnish, taking it about a centimetre up the side of the pot. When dry, the vase should be watertight (you don't see many waterlogged yachts about), though I don't recommend standing it on top of your grand piano until you are absolutely sure that this has worked. (Also, once you've used the yacht varnish in this way you can't of course use the jug for drinks, but just as a vase.) If it still leaks, don't despair . . . I've been using a small glass inside mine and filling that with water instead. One way or another, you won't have to consign it to the dustbin.

Q **I have a large standard lampshade that I want to recover. I have made inquiries locally, but to no avail.**

A Not many people do this sort of work, which is probably why you have had trouble tracking someone down, and it can be expensive. Contact the Association of Master Upholsterers and Soft Furnishers, Frances Vaughan House, 102 Commercial Street,

Newport, Gwent, NP9 1LU, telephone 01633 215454. They will try to put you in touch with someone in your area. There is also a company based in London that can make shades to order: Ann's, 34a/b Kensington Church Street, London W8 4HA, telephone 020 7937 5033. They can deal with an order by post if you send dimensions and details of the materials required.

Q **When my mother was a child she was given a cuddly lion by her father as a present from a trip abroad. When I was growing up this lion, which is about 3 feet long, would stand guard by her bedroom door. Recently I noticed that it was missing and when I asked about it, was told that a moth had got in. I would love to have it repaired for her and wondered if you know of a company who could do the work. I think it must be over 60 years old and made of a similar fabric as early teddy bears.**

A You must move quickly – I can't bear to think of your mother being unguarded all this time. I bet her lion has been as supportive of her over the years as my rather battered-looking teddy has been of me. The Royal School of Needlework, telephone 020 8943 1432, have a commercial workshop that may well be able to undertake this sort of repair. They suggest that you send them a photo of the lion, plus a description of the damage, and they will be able to give you a quote for the work. Write to them at Apartment 12A, Hampton Court Palace, East Molesey, Surrey KT8 9AU. (Sounds the right sort of address to send the king of the beasts to, doesn't it?)

Q We have just moved into a rented house, complete with curtains. I do not want to sell my own curtains, but I'm not sure how to store them effectively to prevent any damage.

A To avoid discoloration it is important that you exclude light and damp, and avoid condensation. I'd try padding and folding them with acid-free tissue, then wrapping in brown paper.

Q I have been entrusted with my daughter's piano but the only place to keep it is in an unheated room that has a slightly damp atmosphere. Will this damage it? I once heard that keeping an ordinary light bulb burning inside might help, but later heard that this can do even more harm.

A You're right to be cautious – the piano 'doctors' I've consulted say that any extremes of humidity (either very dry air in centrally heated houses or very damp air as in your unheated room) are the real killers because they make the wood expand and contract – apparently plain old cold is fine. A bulb would indeed cause damage: instead they recommend that you buy something called a damp chaser, which is an electrical element that acts as a dehumidifier – you just plug it in under the piano. They cost around £10 and are available from most piano shops.

Jane Asher's

HOME CRAFTS

Q **I need to make a quick fairy costume for my three year-old for a party. How can I make something cheap and pretty that isn't too precious to get covered in jelly and cake?**

A Did you know that you can sew crepe paper and lavatory paper? It gathers up beautifully on a sewing machine and looks very effective. Use a swimsuit, ballet leotard or vest and knickers as a base. Choose some pretty pink and white crepe paper and loo paper and ruffle it up into lengths under the machine, using a long stitch. Use the longer crepe paper for the skirt and simply tack lengths of it to the swimsuit around the waist and hips in different coloured layers, then add frills of the loo paper around the neck and armholes. Two chiffon-type scarves tacked down the centre back and attached to elastic round the wrists make lovely floaty wings that she can flap up and down; a few scrumpled paper flowers sewn on to a hairband make a pretty headdress. Glue a cut-out cardboard star to the top of a cheap wooden plant cane, spray it silver – and you've the perfect wand.

Q Please could you tell me how to make those clove-studded dried oranges that seem to be so popular nowadays as Christmas decorations?

A Pomanders like this have been made since the 16th century. Simply press the cloves in lines into the orange, using a small knitting needle or skewer first if necessary, and put them somewhere warm (an airing cupboard if you have one) for two or three weeks to harden. Slices of orange are very fashionable now too: dry them for between 4 and 6 hours in a very cool oven, then tie them to the tree with raffia, or thread them on to a knotted piece of string with some cinnamon sticks, nuts and ribbon. Small fresh oranges, clementines or kumquats, with or without the studded cloves, look terrific too – and should last the 12 days of Christmas. You can always add a few drops of essential oil of clove, frankincense or ginger if you want them to smell as Christmassy as they look.

Q I bet you've never been asked this by a man before, but is there a foolproof way to arrange flowers? I'm rather cack-handed but terribly house-proud and would like to impress the odd friend who comes round to visit. I'm too embarrassed to ask anyone I know.

A You can ask the florist to arrange cut flowers in what is known as a 'tied bunch', then you don't have to do anything at all – not even untie them – but simply plonk them in a vase full of water. If you want to arrange your own it's worth investing in a selection of containers of different sizes and shapes, as even a simple bunch

Jane Asher's

of daffs, for instance, can look very smart if cut down and put generously into a square glass vase. If you don't want to get into florist's foam and chicken wire and all that stuff, then I can recommend a good trick I learnt from a professional – buy a length of Cellophane from a florist (I tried clingfilm but it just isn't the same) and cram it into a glass vase before you arrange the flowers. It looks like crushed ice or pieces of crystal in the water and holds the stems beautifully. You could also use the cellophane that greetings cards and so on are wrapped in.

Q **How do you stop dried lavender from shedding its flower heads? I like to bunch it and dry it, but it always ends up dropping bits all over the floor.**

A Having spoken to flower experts Forever Flowering, it seems that there really are no guarantees with lavender – it always drops a certain amount of its tiny flowers – but the flowers are packed together so tightly that losing a few shouldn't drastically alter the look of your bunch. The main disadvantage is that you'll have to vacuum more often. Some people suggest spraying the bunch with hair spray, artists' spray mount or a special florists' sealer, as well as making sure that the lavender is dried as slowly and gently as possible in the first place.

Q I have collected and dried some poppy heads and would like to colour them. How do I go about this?

A It is fairly straightforward to do – just buy some spray paint (you can get a good variety of colours) and gently spray all over the poppies, trying not to be too 'heavy-handed' as you do it.

Q Someone told me that beanbags are all the rage again. I loved them as a kid and would like to make a couple for my children's playroom but I can't find a suitable sewing pattern. Do you know how it's done? I don't want to end up knee-deep in polystyrene chips.

A *The Hamlyn Book of Soft Furnishings* (Hamlyn, £25) shows you how to make beanbags. But you're right to be concerned about the polystyrene – my craft experts say you should proceed with absolute caution. This is because the bag's inner liner needs to be particularly strong, otherwise any escaping polystyrene beads would pose a great danger to children, so it's a question of making the beanbag shape twice over for each one. Bearing this in mind, you may want to buy them ready-made to the correct safety standards.

Q I'd like to make my eiderdown into a duvet. Is it easy to do myself?

Jane Asher's

I don't think it's a task I'd like to take on myself, but you will find that most reputable dry cleaners offer this service now.

What do you think is the best way to put a cover on a duvet?

Feelings can run quite high on this one. My own method (and I don't claim it's the best) is one that I picked up from my sister. I turn the cover inside out, then reach right into it and grab the two far corners. Then I pick up two corners of the duvet through the cover and simply shake the whole thing violently until the cover turns back the right way round again onto the duvet. Others prefer to take one corner of the duvet and put into one corner of the cover, peg it with a clothes peg, repeat with the other three corners . . . and shake. The Swedes, way ahead of us in duvet technology, now have cut-off corners on their duvet covers, making it easy to hold the duvet inside the covers and shake into place.

Q After a busy summer when we went on a three-week holiday and attended a christening and two family weddings, we have amassed hundreds of photographs that have many happy memories. The problem is that there are just too many to put into an album. What would you suggest?

A Why not be wildly creative and cover some old shoeboxes with fabric remnants, old rolls of wallpaper or sheets of wrapping paper? They'll cost next to nothing but will look a million dollars, especially if you coordinate them with a room scheme or theme them according to their contents – the box of wedding pictures could be covered in silk and the holiday ones could be decorated with shells. Include one photograph on the top somewhere in your scheme, so you know what's inside. Then add labels and card indexes if you're feeling terribly organized – they'll help you to remember dates and places in years to come.

Q My wife always laughs at the mess I make when I try to wrap presents. I'm determined to impress her this year. Where do I start?

A With a bit of plain brown paper, raffia and a luggage label some people can make a gift look amazingly stylish and professional. I think one is or isn't a natural wrapper. I'm not, but I've learned from many of the experts I've worked with and I'm getting better. One trick with oddly-shaped presents to prevent them ending up looking like bags of washing is to put them in boxes first. This will make the job far easier. The second very important tip is not to

Jane Asher's

use too much paper. Cut it down until it neatly covers the box without too much spare that needs tucking or folding and you'll find it'll be far easier to cope with (and save paper). There are several good craft books that will give you lovely ideas for decorating your own paper and gift tags, but if you're seriously determined to impress your wife, why not cheat? Most shops provide a gift-wrapping service. Just pop in to somewhere where you know you'll find something she'll love, then put your gifts in their capable hands. Whether you own up to the truth about who wrapped it I leave to you.

PETS

Q I've been wanting to buy a Jack Russell for ages, but I spend several months at a time in France with friends and would prefer to be able to take the dog with me rather than leave him in kennels. I hear that dogs' passports are going to be available soon – but have you any idea when?

A Apparently, the aim is to have an alternative to quarantine in place by 2001. However, there will be some sort of pilot scheme launched during 2000 which will probably involve guide dogs and hearing dogs, as well as pets that are leaving the country for longer than a conventional holiday. Depending on how much time you intend to spend living it up with your friends, you may be able to get in on this. Anyway, watch the press for more details as they develop – the scheme is bound to attract a lot of publicity when it gets the green light.

Q Can one house-train a rabbit?

A Rabbits make good house pets, and in most cases it is possible to litter-train them. Put the rabbit in the litter tray as soon as it has eaten, and within a few days to a few weeks it should be litter-trained. It is a good idea not to let rabbits into bedrooms, and not to keep them in the house if you have babies or toddlers around.

Jane Asher's

Q

My partner and I have a pedigree rag doll kitten which now regards my girlfriend as her mother and follows her around the flat like a shadow. We are woken by her at first light every morning and she will only eat food that's freshly put down for her. It seems as if the cat is running our lives. What can we do?

A

Aaah – she sounds really sweet. But to let her run your lives is probably going a bit too far. Have you tried speaking to the British Rag Doll Cat Club? Lorna Wallace, the secretary, tells me that the kind of behaviour your cat displays is one of the main reasons why people like this particular breed. Being very affectionate and following you around the house as if they were glued to your feet is, apparently, just in their nature. As for the early morning waking problem, Lorna suggests blacking out the bedroom window or, of course, just insisting that the cat sleep in a nice cosy basket in the kitchen instead. Lorna also reckons that your cat might be less fussy about its food if you gave her one of the specialist dried foods instead of canned meat. If it's all too much for you, the club does offer a re-homing service as a last resort, but I think the sight of the accusative, imploring eyes (from both of them) as she was dragged out of your girlfriend's arms would be very hard to take. The British Rag Doll Cat Club is on 0141 956 1691.

Q My parents are coming up to 65 and are intending to buy a puppy. They have an 11-year-old Labrador and say they want to have another to replace her when she goes. This is the last thing they need, just as they are retired and starting to get more independence again.

A I think they are being very sensible. Some dear friends of mine lost a pet they'd had for many years and they were utterly bereft. They took a lot of persuading to get another one as they felt they could never love it as much, but they did indeed become just as besotted as before. Part of the fun of your parents' retirement will be having more time to enjoy their dog and go for longer walks, and if having a younger one now will save a little of the heartache that losing the 11-year-old will bring, it can only be a good thing. Just be ready to receive two dogs into your home when they visit.

Jane Asher's

PESTS

Q It's that time of year when spiders come marching into the house as if they own the place. Any suggestions on keeping them out?

A Although I'm quite fond of spiders, October is the only time my good-natured, 25-year-old daughter turns into a whirl of outraged fury at the invasion of her room by these harmless creatures. London Zoo's spider man, Craig Walker, says it's something of an illusion that huge spiders suddenly appear in the house at this time of year. They've actually been here all the time, sitting quietly under the bath, turning into big grown-up spiders (but I'm not telling my daughter that). Autumn is the peak time for males to mature, which makes them abandon their webs and go looking for a mate. So there aren't necessarily more spiders, it's just that they're bigger and more mobile than at any other time of year. Sadly for arachnophobes, it's pretty irrelevant to start looking for ways to keep them out: they share your home with you year-round and that's that. The best you can do is live and let live for a month or so, safe in the knowledge that male spiders die out after mating which means you won't have to look another one in the eye for at least 12 months.

Q Help! We've got mice – do I get Rentokil in, or is there a kinder solution?

A The most important preventative action is not to leave bits of food around: a child in particular tends to be a mouse's best friend, leaving interesting crumbs in corners and half-eaten biscuits in waste baskets. Once mice are well established it can be very hard to get rid of them, and you may indeed be well advised to call in the professionals. I have a horror of mouse-traps: there's something about coming down in the morning to find the grisly evidence of one's murderous plans of the night before that is very upsetting. It's not that I'm totally opposed to killing of any kind at any time – after all, I eat meat, wear leather and no doubt dispatch a few million house dust mites every time I hoover the carpet – but I do try to avoid outright cruelty if there's an alternative, and would rather shoo away a fly than swat it. We used to have loads of mice in the house, and the only thing that finally got rid of them was when we got a cat as a pet. For several years that worked wonderfully, but since finding one of our children was allergic to cats we've been a feline-free zone. The mice haven't yet returned, but it must be only a matter of time before the news spreads: I picture them gathering in the wainscot, planning their comeback.

Jane Asher's

Q Every morning I am woken up by pigeons clambering around on top of the dormer window in my bedroom. I could swear they're wearing hobnailed boots they make such a racket. While I don't wish the birds any harm, I would rather not be disturbed so early and so regularly and was wondering whether it is possible to buy the sort of spikes that you see fitted on ledges in railway stations.

A I was just about to give you some recipes for pigeon kebabs when I realized that the spikes are to deter the birds rather than to skewer them. They seem to be an excellent solution, as apparently the birds simply sense that they won't have a very comfortable perch and fly off elsewhere. (Maybe they could be developed for spare bedrooms in case of hovering in-laws?) You can buy these anti-roosting devices by post from Crownguard, who supply kits that include the spikes, sealant, and full instructions. Cost depends on the area you need to cover: enough spikes and glue for 5 metres costs £52, while a 20-metre pack is £180. Both prices include VAT and p & p. Call 020 8959 4525 to order. A cheaper (but less attractive) alternative, is to fix a plastic carrier bag to your window sill or roof – and let the flapping of the bag discourage the birds from perching there.

Q Having recently moved house, I find that we have inherited some carpet beetles in our light woollen carpet. I understand that these are becoming more commonplace in our modern homes, but I would love to know how to get rid of them.

A We share our homes (and our bodies) with a remarkable selection of other creatures – I do recommend a visit to the Natural History Museum if you want to know more – but when they become too obvious or destructive then one really has to act. Carpet beetles look like miniature ladybirds but are orange, white and black (sounds cute!) and their larvae have white bodies with black hairs (on second thoughts . . .). They feed on animal fibres of various sorts including wool, feathers, skin cells, hair, your butterfly collection or the odd dead bird in the attic. The beetles are common outside, but can fly into the house at the drop of a hat through open windows and start work on your carpets – you'll notice small bald areas as if an insect-sized lawn mower has been busy underneath tables or in corners that don't get cleaned so often. Most modern buildings have a certain number of beetles that are actually quite helpful in clearing up the odd bit of debris here and there, but if you've become aware of them it's a job for Rentokil pest control (see your phone book for their local number). You'll need to do the most thorough spring clean you've ever done and they'll apply an insecticide to affected areas. Sometimes floorboards need to be raised too in order to treat the spaces underneath. There's no quick fix, I'm afraid: the only other option is to invite David Attenborough over to make a programme in your living room.

Q I think I've got a birds' nest in my chimney. What can I do to prevent them coming back this spring – or do you think I'm being cruel?

A You'd be far more cruel to light a fire in the grate. Call in the chimney sweep now – anything that's up there will be removed in the process, and if you do it quickly the birds won't have started nesting yet. Ask the sweep to fit a guard to the top to prevent it happening again. Then perhaps you should put extra food on the bird table to make amends for bulldozing the family home.

GARDENING

Q It's September and my summer window boxes are looking very sorry for themselves. I usually just stick in some winter-flowering pansies, but I think I'm being boring.

A Thousands of pansies are planted up and down the land in autumn and left there until the wall flowers take over the following spring, so you're not alone. (And it's amazing the way they just keep on flowering, isn't it? There's usually a very good reason why something has been so successful for so long.) To make a change you could choose plants that give foliage colour – as well as being frost-resistant, they are just as bright and cheery in the depths of winter, and will also give a window box architectural interest. A striking blue-and-yellow scheme could be created using the blue-tinged grass called Festucaovina Glauca with a yellow-leaved eunonymous. And for those of us who still love the bright colours of the pansies, a few can always be planted between the foliage. At the very least I would plant some bulbs in the soil a couple of inches beneath whatever you decide on, as it's a wonderful surprise in the spring when a few daffodils or hyacinths push their way up between the flowers.

Jane Asher's

Q How can I remove large tree stumps from my garden? They can't be taken out with a stump grinder because they are next to a wall, but an ancient gardening books suggests drilling them out, impregnating them with saltpetre and burning them. Is this on?

A Guy Barter of the Royal Horticultural Society at Wisley suggests the saltpetre method is indeed possible but is a lengthy process. It can take weeks for it to soak through the stump, then the equivalent of a whole summer to dry out before burning can begin. Because of your wall, the only other option is to remove them mechanically – attach a winch to the stumps and haul them out (checking first that the wall can cope). Guy suggests getting expert advice first from the Arboricultural Association – they have a list of registered members in your area who can come on site to see what's what. Call them on 01794 368717.

Q I live in a second floor flat and really miss having a garden, especially when all the spring bulbs are out. I look at other people's gardens through green eyes. Although I treat myself to a bunch of flowers each week this gets expensive, so can you suggest any other ways to brighten up my life?

A What about a window box? As they're enjoyed by those both inside and outside the house, they give double the pleasure of indoor plants and as they're so small you can create a whole miniature garden for very little cost. And if you grow herbs in them among the flowers, you can simply lean out of the window to gather in your harvest of chervil or whatever. If windowsills are out, then a large basket filled with pots of polyanthus and daffodils will last for some time (don't bother to plant them; just put the plastic flower pots next to each other and cover with a bit of bought moss if you like). When they're finished you can give them to a friend with a garden. Plenty of pot plants are happy indoors, and don't forget good old leafy houseplants, which will cheer up the flat all year round. Another suggestion might be to develop an interest in bonsai gardening. You can now find several books on the subject that will help you make a tiny scenic garden indoors.

Q **My husband and I hope to move from our tiny second-floor flat to somewhere bigger with (if I get my way) a garden. The problem is that he thinks that gardening is a waste of time and effort, while I think that it would be bliss to have a house with a little plot where we could sit and eat our breakfast on a hot day. The places we have seen don't have acres and acres, just a little patch of lawn and some flower beds round the edge – I reckon an afternoon's work every other weekend should keep it in order. Do you think I am being unrealistic or is he being a spoilsport?**

A Surely the big question is whether you really feel you want to do all the work in the garden on your own? Your other half is being very honest about not wanting to take it on, and you don't want to end up feeling resentful if he doesn't help out, even though he's bound to start enjoying the 'sitting and eating' part of it. Perhaps he feels like a parent does when a young child begs for a pet and swears he'll always clean out that hamster cage or walk that dog:

Jane Asher's

you just know you're going to end up doing it yourself. And don't be fooled by too many dreams of hot days in the garden – it's weeding in the rain and digging the beds in the freezing wind that are going to be the challenging bits: there's more to gardening that picking roses in a floppy hat. But if you don't mind the work, it will give you more pleasure and satisfaction than almost any other hobby – as long as you know what you're in for.

Q I don't have a greenhouse and can't afford a special propagator but would love to grow some unusual flowers for my small garden. Any ideas?

A The best bit of gardening for me is growing flowers from seed: the sense of achievement is out of all proportion to the work involved, and it never fails to make me marvel at the complexity and drama of biology. It's really worth investing in a few plastic seed trays and a bag of compost. My method is then to fill a tray with compost, soak it thoroughly and let it drain a few minutes. Sprinkle the seed on top and press it gently down, covering it with a little more soil if the packet says so, then put the tray into a plastic swing-bin liner. This is the perfect size for covering the tray completely and leaving enough plastic to fold over at the end and tuck under the tray. Put it on a sunny windowsill and you'll find it'll need very little watering – just shake the top of the plastic occasionally so that the condensation drops onto the soil. (If the seeds need darkness to germinate, just use a black bag). As soon as there's any sign of life take the tray out of the bag.

Tricks of the Trade

Q My beautiful roses are infested with green fly, but I hate to use too many sprays. Have you come across any other methods?

A Soapy water is supposed to be as effective as the chemical sprays, but you'll have to use it regularly. Or you could try what a friend of mine used to do – she kept them at bay by aiming a fierce spray of water at the roses. And of course if you see any ladybirds in the garden make sure you're extremely friendly and welcoming to them – they're the best green fly-dispatchers of all.

Q I have a very small courtyard and thought I'd fill it with pots of flowers this year, but my work takes me away for several days at a time. I hate to have to ask my neighbours to come and water for me, but if we have a sunny summer I'm worried that I'd come back to find dead plants in the pots.

A There are watering systems you can install (a version of perforated hoses) and put on a timer, but for a few pots it hardly seems worth it. I should try the new type of compost made especially for hanging baskets and pots: it contains some of those strange jelly-like granules that absorb loads of moisture and mean the pots need far less frequent watering. You'll find it in all the garden centres.

Jane Asher's

Q I have a lean-to with a plastic corrugated roof which is heated with a Calor gas fire. The roof is always getting condensation on the inside, and as we don't really want a shower when we're relaxing I wondered what we could do.

A Condensation is caused when moist air comes into contact with a cold surface, so you have either to make the air drier (by increasing ventilation, drying clothes outside, leaving lids on pans and making sure tumble driers are properly ventilated) or make your home warmer (by insulating and keeping low background heating on at all times). What you should never do is use bottled gas heaters – these put a lot of extra moisture into the air. For a set of four information sheets on tackling damp and condensation in the home, send a cheque for £7.50 (made payable to CRC) to Construction Research Communications Ltd, 151 Rosebery Avenue, London EC1R 4GB.

Q Can you please help my mother to enjoy her new conservatory? She had imagined it would be a lovely place where she could sit and look out at the garden, nicely cocooned away from the heat of the sun and the chill of the wind. Unfortunately, having had the small conservatory built around her kitchen, even the mildly sunny days we have had so far this year are enough to make it so hot that she isn't comfortable sitting in it. Is there anything (other than blinds) that won't cost a fortune that would keep it cool so she can enjoy the garden and birdlife in comfort?

A Your poor Mum – who'd have thought it would be too hot in our climate? There are some ideas to try though: the extremely helpful Glass and Glazing Federation suggest fitting a window in the roof that opens thermostatically or mechanically. Another variation would be to install some ventilation in the ridge – call Ultraframe on 01200 443311 for details. A simpler solution, which can be very effective, is to apply solar tinted film directly to the conservatory glass to deflect the heat: details from the Applied Film Group on 020 7403 7177. Further help can be obtained from the specialist conservatory division of the Glass and Glazing Federation on 020 7207 5873.

SELLING

Q Is there a demand for semi-precious stones? I have inherited some necklaces, brooches and rings in aquamarine, topaz and amethyst, all dating from the 1920s and 1930s. I would really like to sell them but don't know how to go about it.

A You may be sitting on a small fortune. Apparently, you should take this inheritance seriously, as aquamarines, for example, are in fact gems rather than semi-precious stones and so can be worth rather a lot of money. What's more, they tell me that the twenties and thirties are currently the most sought-after eras for jewellery of this sort, which is likely to make your pieces even more valuable. To sell them, the advice is to use an auction house rather than private shops or dealers, as an auctioneer will always be on your side: the more they sell your jewellery for, the more commission they make.

Q I used to collect beer mats and match boxes, but have recently moved to a smaller house and feel the time has come to get rid of them. I can't bear to throw them away – can I sell them?

A I think the best thing for you to do to sell your collection of beer mats and match boxes would be to contact a local auction house (check your Yellow Pages). They will be able to advise you of their worth and give you an idea of potential interested parties.

Q I can't wear my mink coat now, for obvious reasons, but I am loath to throw it away as it is so valuable. Where can I sell it?

A A company called Gale Furs runs fur auctions in London every Saturday. They offer free valuation and take 15% commission on sales. They are at 65 Regents Park Road, London, NW1 8XD, telephone 020 7722 5870.

COOKING & ENTERTAINING

When I was first married I would spend hours in the kitchen slaving away over a hot stove to produce three or four complex courses for a dinner party, and then spend the whole evening in a state of tension, torn between trying to enjoy our guests and knowing I should be back in the kitchen basting the joint or draining the vegetables. Once I had children I was forced to change, and our entertaining inevitably became much more simple and relaxed in every way – and far more enjoyable. I still love to cook, but there are ways of making it quicker and easier, especially for informal meals. And on the few occasions when I want to be more formal, I have discovered over the years all sorts of tricks for making the evening special and memorable while still managing to keep myself relatively calm and happy.

Planning ahead is crucial. This doesn't mean you have to work to endless complex schedules, but a simple list or two of what needs to be done (and when) can stop you feeling panicky. The more advance preparation you can do, the better – try to cook at least one course the day before, and don't plan to cook new dishes without trying them out on friends or family beforehand. You can always serve just one course that needs cooking: choose something like parma ham and melon for a first course and cheese and fruit to finish.

If something does go wrong in the kitchen, don't panic: most disasters can be rescued. A 'split' sauce can usually be saved by adding a bit of cream and whisking at high speed; a burnt roast can have the outside cut off and sliced up out of sight of the guests; overcooked vegetables can be blended with butter and cream and served as an elegant purée. Undercooking can be harder to solve, especially if it's meat or poultry:

it may mean a quick trip to the fish and chip shop rather than poisoning your guests.

If the house needs tidying up (and ours always does!) do it early in the day, before work if necessary, as rushing around at the last second collecting up socks or plastic tractors and hoovering the floor can leave you a bit flushed and breathless when the bell goes. Even better, try to lay the table ahead as well: anything that doesn't need to wait will be a bonus if it's got out of the way as soon as possible. There's always more to do on the night than you think.

Above all, once you've done all you can, try to relax and enjoy the occasion – guests are never going to notice if things aren't perfect, but they will notice if their host or hostess is stressed, anxious and guilty.

Entertaining is meant to be fun, after all.

SPECIAL INGREDIENTS

Q I love mangoes. They remind me of exotic holidays and I've read that they are very good for you. But whenever I try to peel them I end up with juice dripping down my arms and shreds of the flesh still firmly attached to the stone. What am I doing wrong?

A For a start, it's worth buying a large mango which has a bigger proportion of flesh to stone, as it's easier to deal with and is better value. If the mango is very ripe, don't bother peeling it, just cut down either side of the slim stone with a very sharp knife. You will get quite a lot of flesh left sticking to the stone, which is best eaten by the cook with her fingers, then scoop out the rest from each half with a spoon. If you want peeled chunks, cut down either side of the stone as before and peel the two sections carefully before chopping into little cubes. You can also serve half mangoes in their skins scored into squares and turned inside out to be eaten with the fingers. You're right about the health benefits: my spies tell me that one cup of mango slices gives about three-quarters of the adult daily requirement of vitamins A and C.

Q I have root ginger and ginseng and don't know how to get the best use from them. I tried using my food processor, to no avail.

A No, I shouldn't let them anywhere near the food processor. Simply peel them with a sharp knife and either grate them on the small side of a cheese grater or chop finely with a knife. Fresh ginger is delicious used in any recipe in place of dried, and is essential in Oriental cookery. Many people also swear by ginger tea: pop a few slices in a little boiling water and sip to ease a sore throat, clear the head and help the circulation. As for ginseng, all sorts of claims have been made for it, from increasing life span to curing memory loss, but I find the taste so disgusting that I'm tempted to opt for a shorter, more forgetful life.

Q **In the village where I live there is an abundance of wild garlic. I would love to know if I can use it in cooking, and if so, what I could make?**

A Yes, you can cook with wild garlic. The leaves can be picked from spring right through to autumn, and are good in salads, soups or as a vegetable. Unlike the usual garlic (what should I call it – tamed? Raised in captivity?) wild garlic has normal herbaceous roots, not bulbs, so you only use the tops. The flowers aren't particularly dramatic but won't hurt you in any way, so you could use them to decorate the edge of the plate or something if you fancy it.

Q Following a holiday in Italy I am addicted to sun-dried tomatoes and get through several packets a week. Is there any way I can buy plum tomatoes and dry them myself this summer? I know they won't be kissed by the Mediterranean sun, but Cornwall can get pretty hot so I'd like to give it a bash if you can tell me how.

A I'm writing this a couple of weeks away from Midsummer Day – and it's wet, windy and cold. I'm afraid Newquay-dried tomatoes are out of the question: you'd spend most of your time bringing them in like the washing.

Q I have been recommended to eat lots of spinach for its vitamins. Can you suggest some recipes that will make it more appealing?

A The taste of spinach is wonderful, but it can make your mouth feel very dry, so I always like to add a bit of moisture back into it once it's cooked. Either I sprinkle it with olive oil and lemon as the Italians do, or I make a white sauce, with or without cheese, and pour that over it. It's also fabulous blended with cream and nutmeg or egg, then used in quiches and filo pies. You'll be Popeye before you know it.

Q My herb garden flourishes during the summer, but come autumn I feel bereft. I tried drying some sprigs last year but they turned out to be nothing special. Could using herb butter instead be the answer?

Jane Asher's

A Yes, it works very well: it saves time when you need herbs for cooking and freezes perfectly. To make it, soften some unsalted butter by mashing it in a bowl with a fork. Mix in some finely chopped fresh herbs – coriander, basil or tarragon, for example. Shape the butter into a log and wrap in clingfilm, then foil. Freeze for up to one month. Butter can also be flavoured with pesto, citrus zest or sun-dried tomatoes, then frozen in the same way. Simply cut off enough to put on top of meat, salads or pasta and you can give a meal an instant lift. The other option for preserving herbs is to chop them as before, then freeze them in a little water in ice-cube moulds. When you want to add some to soups, sauces or stews, simply decant one of the cubes and throw straight into the pan. Unless you have huge quantities of herbs that you can't bear to waste, I agree that drying is not worth it – the freeze-dried herbs in the shops will probably taste better than yours and save a lot of bother.

Q I have a great deal of mint in the garden and would like to make some mint jelly – do you have a recipe? I do freeze mint and use that during the winter, but jelly would be much nicer.

A I never think frozen herbs are particularly successful, except when chopped and frozen with water in ice-cube trays to add directly to soups and sauces or into drinks like Pimms or gin and tonic. I love mint jelly and it's really easy: all herb jellies are basically apple jellies flavoured with mint, rosemary, thyme and so on. Chop up some windfalls or cooking apples and put them in a preserving pan. To each kilo (2 lb) add 100 ml (3½ fl oz) white wine vinegar and enough water barely to cover the fruit. Add a few large sprigs of mint and simmer until the fruit is very soft, then strain it through a jelly bag, leaving it overnight to drip. There's so much natural pectin in apples that you don't have to worry about boiling times, temperatures or special jam sugar – it will set beautifully into a lovely green, clear jelly. If you've still got extra mint (and it really does spread in the garden, doesn't it?) try making a sandwich-spread from equal quantities of raisins and mint, processed or minced with a little hot water.

Q I know olive oil is healthy, but which do I buy: olive oil, pure olive oil, virgin olive oil or extra virgin olive oil?

A It depends on what you want to use it for and on your own taste. For salads and where the taste of the oil will be an important part of the dish, it's worth buying extra virgin. Even in this category there are many different types, some of which are a bit peppery for me, and there are cold-pressed, first pressings, vintages and goodness knows what. If you go to a good Italian delicatessen then they may let you taste a few to see what you like. I buy mine in a large can (bigger outlay but more economical in the long run) from Gastronomia Italia in Victoria. For general use, a lighter non-virgin one is better and cheaper, but you should certainly always go for 'pure' – there's no point in buying a mix. I'm such a fan of olive oil that I cook almost everything with it instead of butter – even a white sauce works brilliantly, is easier to make and presumably healthier too. There are plenty of other oils to try too, from pumpkin seed to walnut. If you'd like to learn more, I've just bought myself a great little book, full of information and recipes, by chef Mark Emmerson: *A Feast of Oils* (Thorsons, £8.99).

Q **What is the difference between fromage frais and crème fraiche? I am not sure when I should use one or the other, and my recipe books from only a few years ago don't even mention them.**

A This really made me think. I love them both, but up until now have always chosen which to use more on instinct than through any informed decision. The fact is that crème fraiche (a type of soured cream) is considerably higher in fat than fromage frais (which is really a soft cheese). Although they are interchangeable in most recipes, you need to decide how rich and creamy you want your result to be. Even if you buy the low-fat type of crème fraiche, you'll see that it's still higher in fat content than the fromage frais. I did a blind tasting with several pots and a teaspoon on a rather limited sample of one 15-year-old son, and for taste and texture the crème fraiche won every time, but for lighter dishes and those trying to keep to a low-fat diet the fromage frais makes an excellent alternative.

Q My dear late wife was a brilliant cook and I learned much from her so I don't starve, but cooking potatoes with every dinner is beginning to pall and I would love to try rice. How much rice and water would I need for one person, and which spices could I add for colour and flavour? (I'm not a great lover of garlic.) Also, what are basmati, patna and wild rice used for?

A I'm sure your wife would be proud to know about your cooking efforts and how she inspired you. Yes, plain rice can get a bit bland, although it depends very much on the type. Patna and basmati are both long grain and best for most savoury uses. For risottos you need a medium grain, such as arborio, and for puddings a short grain (usually known as pudding rice, for obvious reasons). Wild rice isn't actually rice at all, but a type of grass seed: it's delicious but very expensive. My favourite of the long grains is basmati, and the brown is especially good. Fifty grammes (2 oz) or about half a cupful of rice will be plenty for one serving with twice the amount of water. If you want to add salt, add it after cooking. You can always add a stock cube to the cooking water or even one of those new cubes made specially for flavouring rice, or fry up a few onions and spices in some oil or butter and mix it into the cooked rice. If you like the taste of curry then you could add a little ready-made curry paste to the onion and cook it for a while before adding it to the rice. Chopped fresh herbs (parsley or coriander in particular) added at the last minute are delicious – you'll find once you get brave there's really no end of ingredients you can add. It's worth taking a few good vegetarian or Asian cookery books out of the library, as they'll be full of ideas.

Q

Is it humanly possible to make supermarket basil in pots survive more than 24 hours? And what can I do with it other than chop it up in salads?

A

I've asked Sainsbury's and they say that you can prolong the plant's life by keeping it in its plastic sleeve and storing it at between 16 and 24°C (60 and 75°F) in a bright spot away from direct sun and draughts. They advise watering from underneath, keeping it moist but not saturated. I too have not had much success so I also talked to Nicholas Turrell, a garden designer, and he says each pot is really many plants crammed in together. This reduces circulation and so plants soon go mouldy and keel over. I have heard of people who have kept their plants alive for up to a year, and there are several tricks to try:

- Remove almost all the plants as soon as you get home, leaving only four or five to grow larger.
- Pick off the top shoots and when the stem gets brown cut it right back and let the new green shoots appear.
- Try growing new plants: place cuttings in a glass of water and replant when the roots are long.

As for cooking with it, basil is not known as the king of herbs for nothing – it has one of the most exquisite smells and tastes in cookery. It's more a question of when *not* to use it. Almost anything involving tomatoes is better with some roughly chopped fresh basil: from soups, salads and sauces to pasta and omelettes. Whizz some up in a blender with some pine nuts, garlic and olive oil, add some grated parmesan and you've the classic Italian pesto which can be used not only as a pasta sauce but also on fish and grilled meat, added to mayonnaise or simply spread on some toasted crusty bread. But my favourite has to be a simple salad of sliced dark red tomatoes topped with extra virgin olive oil, sea salt and chopped basil. Accompanied by a glass of Soave or Orvieto it takes me straight back to holidays in Amalfi.

Q **How do I cook venison? I've never tried it before but my brother has talked me into it and I'm now quite keen.**

A I love venison – and I'm sure you know that it's not only delicious but also extraordinarily healthy, as it has all the benefits of red meat without the cholesterol. You can cook it in just the same way you would a good cut of beef, but bear in mind that it can dry out easily. I enjoy it most in a rich casserole made with plenty of red wine. Adding some juniper berries is traditional, and you can buy them in those little spice jars. Serve with a potato-and-parsnip purée and you've the perfect winter supper.

Q **I have been trying for ages to find out about buttermilk. Is it the same as semi-skimmed milk, is it yoghurt with water, is it a powder? I saw you making Irish soda bread with it on TV recently but I'm still not sure.**

Jane Asher's

A Oh no, it's none of those. It used to be the rather acidic liquid left after churning butter, but it is now made from lactol. It was used in cooking a great deal in the old days, and is still used to make soda bread. Up until recently it's been rather forgotten in the UK, although it has always been widely available in Ireland, and the Americans make all kinds of breads and pancakes with it. I'm pleased to say it's now around again here, and you can buy it in cartons in most good grocers and supermarkets.

Q **I make Hallowe'en lanterns out of turnips every year for my kids, but I am always at a loss to know what to do with the turnip I'm left with once I've hollowed them out. Apart from mash – which reminds me of school dinners – what can I make with it?**

A Perhaps it will remind you less of school if you mix the turnip with other root vegetables. A combination of carrot, turnip and celeriac, mashed with a little sour cream, a pinch of sugar and grated nutmeg, is delicious. And of course, you can substitute turnip for potato in many classic dishes: turnip dauphinoise, turnip croquettes and so on. Turnip chips might be taking things a bit far, though.

Q My father has a White Marseille fig tree in his greenhouse. Unfortunately it produces more fruit than he can eat. Can you suggest any alternative uses for them?

A OK, I'm going to come clean. I had never heard of this fig. I was feeling very inadequate until I discovered that neither Prue Leith nor Sophie Grigson had heard of it either. Eventually I found out that it's an old and well-respected breed (there's a large one in the grounds of Lambeth Palace). Although it's tempting to pick them as soon as they feel soft, it's important to wait until a little drop of syrup oozes from the calyx (the husk) to demonstrate full ripeness. They can be treated just like any other figs – delicious eaten on their own, with cheese or Parma ham, or cooked in compotes and eaten with cream. Sophie suggests looking in a Greek cookery book for one of their wonderful pre-serves, and it might well be worth bottling some: it's easy to do and makes you feel very smug as you arrange the neatly labelled jars on a shelf. Freezing works well, but must be done when the figs are a little under-ripe – the thawing process will give them extra softness. Many cake and biscuit recipes include figs, and the following one is popular with both children and adults:

Fig Fingers

500 g/1.1 lb figs, cooked in a little water and drained
120 g/5 oz porridge oats
120 g/5 oz softened butter
120 g/5 oz plain flour

50 g/2 oz soft brown sugar
1 tsp bicarbonate of soda

Blend the cooked figs in a food processor or blender. Mix all the other ingredients together. Spread half the oat mixture on the bottom of a lined or non-stick pan, add the figs and top with another layer of oat mixture. Bake for 30 minutes in a moderate oven. Allow to cool, then cut into fingers.

Q **I have a quince bush that's covered in fruit. It seems a waste to leave it for the birds, but what on earth can I cook with them?**

A Oh, but you're so lucky! Quince jelly is delicious: look in the jam chapter of any good cookery book and you'll find the recipe. It's very simple as, like crab apples, quinces are full of natural pectin so they set with no problem and turn the most glorious colour. Don't keep it just to spread on bread or toast, either: it has become very trendy to serve quince jelly with cheese as a smart dessert.

Q Every year I make chutney, crumbles and pies with the apples from the tree in my garden. My family will scream if I produce the same again this year.

A You could always juice some of them if you or a friend has an electric juicer (very healthy), or why not be brave and give them all away this year? You solve the glut problem, make someone else happy and at the same time get the smug glow of being a generous giver. And with any luck, after a year off, your family will be crying out for your delicious apple pies. If you can't bring yourself to do it, here are a few simple ideas:

- Cook the sliced, cored and peeled apples with some runny honey and a little lemon juice until soft. Layer the mixture in tall, slender glasses with some luxury muesli that has been cooked in a pan with a little unsalted butter.
- Cook the apples to a puree with 1–2 tablespoons of runny honey and a little lemon juice and place in lightly greased ramekins. Whisk up two egg whites and gradually fold in 125 g/5 oz castor sugar, whisking after each addition, until it makes a stiff meringue. Spoon the meringue over the apple mix and bake at 400°F/200°C/Gas Mark 6 for 10 minutes until just browned.
- Make an apple, walnut and cheese salad – perfect for using up dessert apples. Halve, quarter and core the apples. Sprinkle with a little lemon juice. Melt a little unsalted butter in a pan. Add the apples and pan-fry briskly until just

golden brown. Add a few walnut halves and cook together. Serve with salad leaves scattered with crumbled Wensleydale, Cheshire or Cheddar cheese.

For more inspiration, and recipes for such old English favourites as apple pan dowdy, apple sponge with ginger, apple Charlotte and apple jelly, there are several books devoted solely to apples: *20 Ways to Cook Apples* by Pearl Spooner (Thomas Harmsworth, £3.99) or *Apples: a Book of Recipes* (Lorenz Books, £4.95).

Q **Both my husband and I have heart trouble, so in my wisdom I bought some whole egg replacer. It reminds me of the dried egg my late mum used during the war, but I can't remember exactly what she made with it. Can you suggest any recipes?**

A I am sorry to hear you both have heart trouble – I assume the whole egg replacer has less cholesterol than the real thing? Have you heard of Columbus eggs which are supposed to be positively good for the heart? I buy them in our local supermarket. The chickens are fed on certain grains and seeds that are apparently full of omega-3 oils. I checked with the *Daily Express* doctor Phil Hammond, who thought they might well be worth a try. He also said, interestingly, that he feels the whole business of cutting out eggs can be overdone, and that eating cholesterol doesn't necessarily mean more cholesterol in the arteries: it's more complicated than that (my doctor father used to say exactly the same thing). So it might be worth checking with your doctor anyway.

Meanwhile, I asked my mother about dried egg, as she still has some wartime cookery books (full of Asher parents, this answer). Apparently you mix it with equal amounts of water and then use as normal eggs, but to start you off here are a couple of recipes. I'm NOT giving them in metric for once, as anyone using dried egg is bound to think in imperial measurements, as I still tend to do!

Batter:
1 level teaspoon dried egg
4 oz flour
pinch of salt
½ pint of milk and water

Mix dry ingredients, add sufficient liquid for stiff mixture, beat well, add the rest of the liquid and beat again.

Caramel Custard:
4 level tablespoons sugar
2 tablespoons water
4 dried eggs reconstituted
1 pint of milk
1 level tablespoon sugar

Flavouring

Make a caramel by boiling together the sugar and the water until a dark brown caramel. Pour this into lined cups or moulds. Make the custard with the other ingredients as if for baked custard and add to the moulds. Place the moulds in a shallow pan of cold water. Bake in a moderate oven until set.

FAVOURITE RECIPES

Q A few years ago I saw you demonstrate an easy cake that looked like a Christmas pudding. My children liked it much better than the traditional Yule Log and have asked me to make it again, but I can't remember what kind of icing you used.

A I used a simple all-in-one sponge recipe cooked in a pudding basin and covered it with chocolate ganache, which is simply double cream mixed with melted chocolate, then studded it with a few currants to look like a pudding mix. The 'cream' on top can be made either of melted white chocolate or white chocolate ganache.

Q I have just been on holiday to the West Country and was served the most heavenly but simple pudding – butterscotch sauce on some dreamy local vanilla ice cream. I'm sure it would be easy enough to re-create this at home, if only I knew how to make the sauce.

A If you're not making your own ice cream make sure you buy a good one that uses real cream and vanilla (don't you think non-dairy ice-cream is one of the weirdest ideas? Talk about a contradiction in terms!) Make a simple and delectable sauce by putting 50 g (2 oz) butter, 75 g (3 oz) soft brown sugar, 50 g (2 oz) granulated sugar and 125 g (5 oz) golden syrup in a heavy-bottomed saucepan and heat slowly until the syrup and sugar dissolve.

Jane Asher's

Remove from the heat and stir in 125 ml (4 fl oz) of double cream. As you can see this recipe is very slimming and healthy (and pigs will fly).

Q **I would like to cook some savoury pancakes as a main course on Shrove Tuesday, as I fancy a change from the usual sugar and lemon ones. Do I use the same batter as normal? And can you suggest some tasty fillings?**

A Yes, the same batter will be fine. I use an easy-to-remember formula from Philip Harben, the chef who inspired me as a child. It is 1:3:5 (or 1 egg to 3 oz flour to 5 fl oz milk), adding a splash of water if I want to make thin pancakes. (It doesn't work for metric, of course, so it's 1 egg, 75 g flour and 150 ml of milk to all modern young things). You could use half wholemeal flour if you like and all sorts of interesting fillings. Try ricotta with spinach; cooked minced beef bolognaise; cooked chicken and mushroom; or, for a special occasion, lobster and prawns in a cheese sauce. Put a spoonful in the centre of each pancake, roll them up and put them in an oven-proof dish. Pour over some thick white or tomato sauce, sprinkle with cheese and heat through thoroughly in the oven.

Q I am getting married in four months' time and, in an effort to save some money (the whole thing is costing a fortune) I would like to have a bash at making my own cake. Can I just follow my mum's Christmas cake recipe, double the ingredients, then divide it between three tins? And how far in advance do I need to make it? I am quietly confident about icing it, as I am quite creative and it looks easy enough (though I shouldn't really say that to the queen of cake decorating, should I?) but I don't want it to be a disaster as soon as the knife gets past the pretty bit.

A Strange things happen when you multiply up the ingredients for a recipe: you'd think that by keeping the same proportions you'd simply end up with larger quantities of exactly the same thing, but it doesn't always work that way. You'll need to borrow a good cake decorating book, look up the sizes of your three tins and it'll tell you how many eggs, kilos of flour and sugar and so on that you'll need. If you particularly like your mum's recipe then you should be able to adapt it to the right amounts. Make it as far in advance as possible – not only because the taste will get better as the cake matures, but also because I have a feeling you'll have one or two other things to do between now and the wedding. Wrap the cakes loosely in greaseproof paper and store them in airtight tins, just opening them once a month or so to sprinkle with a little brandy. Use white marzipan to cover them at least a week ahead of the great day, and over that I recommend the roll-out icing if you're not experienced at getting a smooth surface with layers of royal icing. If you need help, advice, cake

Jane Asher's

tin hire or icing equipment of any kind my shop now stocks a complete professional and amateur sugarcraft range – ring 020 7584 6177, or go to the web page: www.sugarcraft.co.uk for more information.

Q I'm having a barbecue next weekend for friends and family and would like to make some non-alcoholic drinks for the children and drivers. I know how to make a fruit punch, but wondered if you had a recipe for home-made lemonade, which I'd imagine would be lovely and summery.

A Home-made lemonade isn't just a wonderful taste of summer – for me it also has echoes of the kind of idyllic, sunny childhoods that only exist in the worlds of Enid Blyton or E Nesbit. When I – occasionally – bring a jug of it out into the garden for the family, it makes me feel for a few moments like a calm, nurturing, old-fashioned mother, instead of the busy, irritable, working mum of reality.

Thinly peel 4 washed lemons (it's worth getting the unwaxed ones for this) and put the rind into a jug with 100–150 g (4–6 oz) of castor sugar. Pour over 1.2 litres (2 pts) of boiling water and stir well. Leave it till it's cold, then strain it and add all the lemon juice. (Makes 4–6 glasses.) I can also thoroughly recommend adding a little elderflower syrup: you can easily buy it ready-made from the supermarket. (Unless of course you really are one of those sicken-ingly perfect people – in which case you'll have a neat little row of labelled bottles home-made from the hedgerows last year.)

Q Could you recommend a good recipe for pease pudding? It's so long since I made one that I can't remember what to do.

A I love pease pudding, and it's not difficult to make. Soak 500 g (1 lb) dried split peas for at least 3 hours, drain them and then simmer them in plenty of water for about 45–60 minutes until tender. Drain again (use the liquid for soup) and then process or sieve the peas into a rough puree. Mix in 50 g (2 oz) butter and 1 large egg, season well and then put into a buttered basin and steam for an hour. Turn it out and serve with boiled ham. In the past it would have been boiled in a cloth with the ham. (My more usual method, which takes all of 5 minutes rather than 5 or 6 hours, is to open a tin of pease pudding, heat it up and stir in a bit of butter and salt and pepper. One of those things that I think is just as good from a can.)

Q How do you make ice cream out of bought custard and those frozen bags of forest fruit?

A Classic ice cream is based on a homemade custard which can take a little time to do. You can indeed cheat with ready-made custard but you'll need to add some cream to get a high enough fat content. Whisk 150 ml (5 fl oz) double or whipping cream until it hangs off the whisk. Fold it into the contents of a 15 oz/375 g can or carton of full-fat custard. Add a little vanilla essence, the frozen fruit (don't defrost it first) and a little icing sugar and place in a plastic container. Freeze, covered, for several hours, stirring from time to time, until firm. Another easy cheat – and delicious in its own right – is to use a Greek-type yoghurt instead of a custard or cream. Just add some fruit or flavouring with sugar and freeze, beating every 10 minutes or so to stop crystals forming. I often make it – it has a sharper, less creamy taste and is very refreshing.

If you want to make ice cream or sorbets quite regularly then it's worth thinking about investing in an ice cream maker: everything goes in at once and you simply switch it on and forget about it.

Q I have lost a recipe for chicken cooked in garlic. All I can remember is that the chicken is cooked in a large crock pot surrounded by 20–25 cloves of garlic and sealed with a pastry lid to keep in all the flavours. When it is cooked the lid is discarded and each person removes a piece of chicken and then dips it into the garlic mush. Potatoes can also be cooked in the same pot.

A Yes, it's delicious and, amazingly, garlic cooked in this way does not taste horribly strong or make you socially unacceptable the next day. I found this particular version on the Internet (any other garlic-loving nerds like me may like to visit it on www.garlicpage.com). Put 40 unpeeled cloves of garlic (yes, 40!) in a casserole and place the chicken on top. Add a bouquet garni, salt and pepper and two cups of chicken stock or white wine. Cover the casserole and cook in a preheated oven at 450°F/230°C/Gas Mark 8 for 1–1½ hours, depending on the size of the chicken, basting once or twice. Add extra liquid as necessary. Serve the chicken, garlic still unpeeled, with some crusty French bread. Slide the skins off the garlic cloves and spread them on the bread.

Q Is it easy to make your own moulded chocolate Easter eggs? I've always wanted to have a go as I think they would make really special presents for the family.

A A little time-consuming and a bit fiddly but, as long as you've got the right equipment, it's not really difficult. I recommend plastic moulds (ring my shop on 020 7584 6177 if you can't find any and we can send you some). Buy couverture or good bakers' chocolate (most supermarkets stock it) and follow the directions carefully when you melt it. Then it's a question of coating the inside of the mould with chocolate, letting it harden and repeating the process twice more until the chocolate is thick enough. It's worth piping a decoration on the outside with some melted white chocolate or royal icing, and adding a name makes it particularly personal and special.

Q I want to roast a boned leg of lamb – can you suggest a stuffing to go with it?

A How about a mint stuffing? Extremely easy to make, fresh tasting, and a natural to go with lamb. Simply fry a chopped large onion in a little oil then mix with 200 g (8 oz) breadcrumbs, 75 g (3 oz) butter, 3 tablespoons chopped parsley and half a cup of chopped

Jane Asher's

fresh mint. Season with salt, pepper and a pinch of sugar and spread over the boned joint. Alternatively, you might like to try the fabulous recipe for marinated butterflied leg of lamb in Nigella Lawson's brilliant book *How to Eat* (Chatto & Windus, £25). It has the great advantage of cooking really quickly and tastes delicious.

Q **I have scoured my wife's cookbooks for a simple recipe for curry sauce, but have had no luck. It's bound to be cheaper than getting meals from our local takeaway, which we do once a week.**

A Well, it depends of course what you mean by curry. The version I make at home, which goes down well with the family, is inevitably very different from a 'proper' one, which involves grinding the spices and combining them in the right proportions for particular dishes and tastes. Some of the ready-made sauces are OK, but a sort of halfway cheat is more economical and tastier: I think the pastes make better sauces than powders and I simply follow the instructions on the back of the jar, improvising as necessary to suit whatever ingredients I have to hand. Choose the type that is nearest to your favourite curry: I go for Korma or Moglai, as I'm a wimp about hot curries and those are both very mild.

Q Have you a recipe for spotted dog? Is it just a suet pudding with raisins in it?

A I've always assumed that spotted dog is the same thing as the more sniggeringly named Spotted Dick. At school it was a regular on our pudding menu, and it was exactly the same as any old currant suet pud but shaped in a long roll rather than being basin-shaped. I am told that the original method of cooking spotted dick was to boil it in a cloth and serve it cut into slices with butter and sugar or treacle. Leftovers were fried in butter the next day, again served with sugar or treacle. Mix together 75 g (3 oz) each of self-raising flour, shredded suet and fresh breadcrumbs with 50 g (2 oz) castor sugar, 150 g (6 oz) currants or raisins and a pinch of salt. Add enough milk to make a soft dough, then shape it into a roll on a floured surface, wrap loosely in greaseproof or silicone paper and then in foil. Steam for 1½–2 hours, put on your gymslip and enjoy it with thick lumpy school custard!

Q Could you please give me a recipe for faggots? My husband has suddenly acquired a taste for them, but none of my cookery books can help.

A Faggots can be made of various types of meat and offal and were popular in the old days for using up the bits and pieces left over when a pig was killed: with so much mass-produced, sanitized food around, one doesn't often see at first-hand those strange innards that are part of many traditional dishes. For good faggots, you'll need a piece of caul fat (ask a good family butcher) and a copy of Jane Grigson's *English Food* (Penguin, £6.99, or try the library). I've never actually cooked them myself.

Q Is it really worth doing home-made mayonnaise, now that the shop ones are so good?

A It depends what you're using it for. The jars of ready-made mayonnaise are perfect for snacks, everyday salads and sandwiches (in fact, a BLT wouldn't taste right with home-made, somehow) but to go with salmon or for a special potato salad I think it's worth making your own, simply because modern gadgets make it so easy. Standing with a whisk and bowl and adding drop by drop used to be a real trial, but with a blender or hand-held electric wand it is fantastically quick and foolproof, and if you use a good olive oil the taste really is fabulous.

Q I recently made bread rolls from a pack of ciabatta mix bought in my local supermarket and was amazed by the wonderful texture and taste. I would like to make my own from scratch but can't find a recipe without hard-to-find ingredients. The Italians must have a simpler formula.

A As I'd never made ciabatta and none of my cookery books listed it, I bought myself *Making Bread at Home* by Tom Jaine (Phoenix, £9.99). It's a wonderful, inspiring book and I shall try lots of recipes from around the world but, as for ciabatta, all I need to do is quote one line from Tom's recipe: 'It's not an easy loaf to make at home.' That's enough for me, thanks, but if you're feeling brave you know where to find it. If you were happy with the results of your packet I should stick to that – some of the shop-bought bread mixes give fantastic results.

Q **A few weeks ago I bought from a supermarket four small sponge cakes that were topped with apricot jam and then covered with chocolate. They were 90% fat free and had a delicious light, texture. Have you a recipe that I could use to give the same kind of cake with a similarly low-fat content?**

A These low-fat things usually contain masses of sugar, so aren't really 'healthy' or 'slimming' at all, unless you're particularly worried about eating fat as such and not about losing weight. My attitude is that cakes are delicious, buttery, sweet, eggy concoctions that should be enjoyed in their original form, and that – unless you have an allergic condition or medical problem that entails avoiding specific ingredients – it's much better to indulge in the real thing occasionally and enjoy it to the full, than to eat a substitute more often.

Jane Asher's

Q Have you got a good recipe for coffee buns? I lost my mother's when I moved house recently and no one seems to know how to make them.

A The problem is that 'buns' is such a wonderfully vague word which can cover everything from little cakes to eclairs, so it's a bit tricky to know just what your mum's were like. Almost any simple cake recipe, from sponge to Madeira, can be flavoured with coffee by making up a very strong solution of black coffee (either instant or freshly ground) and using it as a substitute for some of the liquid. If you want a stronger and more moist result you can pierce the cooked buns with a skewer and drizzle some coffee syrup (coffee simmered with sugar, or buy a ready-made one) over them when they come out of the oven. The following simple, all-in-one recipe has always been popular with my family, so it may be worth a try to see if it's what you're after.

Mix together 75 g (3 oz) self-raising flour, 5 ml (1 tsp) baking powder; 30 ml (2 tbsp) instant coffee powder; 15 ml (1 tsp) cocoa; 100 g (4 oz) soft tub margarine; 100 g (4 oz) castor sugar and two medium eggs. Beat for 2 minutes then spoon into a greased bun tin or paper cases. Bake at 400°F/200°C/Gas Mark 6 for 15–20 minutes. Let the buns cool. Either eat as they are or spread with some icing.

Make the icing by dissolving 10 ml (2 tsp) instant coffee in 15–30 ml (1–2 tsp) of warm water. Add little by little to 100 g (4 oz) icing sugar until it is of spreading consistency and beat well. Spread on to the buns and sprinkle with chocolate flakes.

Q Your Everyday Gingerbread is delicious but too soft to make gingerbread men for my children. How can I adapt it?

A The sort of gingerbread that can be transformed into men (or women – let's not be sexist about our biscuits) is a completely different texture from the cake-type that you've been making. This easy recipe gives a slightly chewy texture and a very rich taste:

Cream 100 g (4 oz) soft margarine and 200 g (8 oz) soft brown sugar in a mixing bowl, then add 200 g (8 oz) plain flour, 1 tsp ginger and 1 tbsp each of warmed golden syrup and black treacle, mixing well. Turn the mixture onto a floured surface and knead lightly with your hands until it comes together as a light, crumbly dough. Chill for half an hour or so if you find it difficult to handle, then roll out to a thickness of about ⅛ inch.

Cut out gingerbread men or other shapes, then add currants for eyes and buttons, pressing them lightly into the dough. Bake for 10 minutes or so in an oven pre-heated to 375°F/190°C/Gas Mark 5, until they are just beginning to brown a little around the edges. Move them onto a rack to cool completely (don't worry if they seem a little soft – they'll harden as they cool). If you like you can decorate the men with a little royal icing, glace cherries, hundreds and thousands and so on.

Q I would like to make ice cream using goat's milk, but have heard that this can be problematic.

A Apparently this is no problem at all. Ascott, who specialize in Goat, Poultry and Dairy Supplies assure me that the following recipe for Goat's Milk Vanilla Ice Cream is delicious.

Infuse a vanilla pod in 1.2 litres (2 pints) of goat's milk and bring it to the boil. Whisk 8 medium egg yolks and 250 g (10 oz) castor sugar, then, stirring all the time, pour on the boiled milk. Put back on the heat and continue to stir until the mixture thickens and coats the back of a spoon, being very careful not to bring it to the boil as the mixture will curdle. Pass through a fine sieve and leave to cool, then put into a shallow dish in the freezer for 30 minutes. Take out and whisk, then replace in the freezer until firm. Before eating, leave the ice cream at room temperature for 10–15 minutes to soften a little.

Among other things, Ascott supply equipment for making your own cheese, yoghurts and butter. Ring them on 01691 690750 or visit their website on www.soft.net.uk/ascott if you're interested.

Q Can you suggest any socially acceptable alternatives to crisps and chocolate that won't make my kids the butt of jokes at school?

A Most supermarkets now stock handy-sized bags of small apples, pears and bananas for lunchboxes. Cute mini-cheeses in pick 'n' mix bags are fun, and mini-pittas filled with tuna and sweetcorn make a change from sandwiches. But surely you needn't totally deprive them of crisps? There are plenty of low-fat, low-salt types – or even vegetable crisps – and the occasional chocolate bar isn't going to do any harm. Some of the so-called healthy snack bars have just as much sugar as chocolate does. It's dangerous to be too one-sided about these things: a relative was determined to bring up her daughter without any sweets; as a result, the child became obsessed with them and is now a sweet addict.

Jane Asher's

PREPARING AND PRESERVING

Q Does papaya lose its goodness if frozen? I have been giving one a day to my daughter who has Cri-du-Chat syndrome, after hearing that the fruit has healing properties. It is really helping – she has stopped being so sickly and is eating much better. My local greengrocer has to buy papayas for me in boxes of 10 but the fruit doesn't keep fresh for 10 days. So scooping out the flesh and freezing it would be a good solution, but only if the goodness remains.

A I am so sorry to hear that your daughter has Cri-du-Chat syndrome. I know a little about it through being a Trustee of Children in Need. It's very interesting that you feel papaya may be helping, and there is certainly no reason why you shouldn't freeze it. I am assured by the British Nutrition Foundation that freezing preserves a lot of the vitamins and minerals in food, but be sure to freeze it as soon as you get it home.

Q The Christmas cake I had made in October and marzipanned in mid-December didn't get iced or eaten. How long can I safely keep it and how should I store it?

A Are you secretly hoping it'll last until next year? The cake itself will indeed stay tasty and moist for several years, but the marzipan will begin to dry out and go hard after a couple of months. If you don't eat in within that time then you'll need to cut away the marzipan and redo it – we often do this to the tops of wedding cakes that are brought back to the shop to be re-iced as christening cakes. Meanwhile, keep the cake in a layer or two of greaseproof paper in an airtight tin and it'll be fine whichever way you decide to use it.

Q I have rented a cottage in the Highlands for a week and would like to stay somewhere overnight on the journey. Usually I take frozen food with me, but is there any way that it would keep in the car for this long? Would placing it in a cool bag surrounded by ice suffice?

A It might be worth turning your freezer temperature right down for a day before you go to make sure the food is really frozen solid, and buy a couple of bags of ice from a supermarket so that you can use plenty to pack around the food. Check it as you stop for the night, and if in doubt replace some of the ice – you can often get it at garages now. An alternative to using ice is to use freezer blocks, packing the box solidly and filling any gaps with bags of frozen peas. Try not to open the box too often on the journey, as this would let warm air in.

Jane Asher's

Q I have a spray of hand-made sugar flowers that were part of the decoration of my granddaughter's wedding cake. Is it possible to keep this for any length of time?

A It'll last for some time just as it is: sugar is, of course, one of the most efficient preservatives around. It will become very hard and brittle and you'll be able to dust it gently just like a china ornament, or keep it in a glass-fronted cupboard in a warm but not damp room. You can use a confectioners' glaze spray, but if any detail has been painted onto the flowers it may make it run – and you really don't gain much anyway. If you can keep it covered – a tiny glass dome is ideal – and out of direct strong light it'll delight you for years, although the colours may fade a little. Small glass domes can be bought from Talbot Designs (020 8346 8515). They do all the domes you see on the lottery draw and sci-fi films, but are happy to do one-off orders like this. Sizes range from 10 cm to 150 cm diameter. The smallest cost £12 plus VAT and p & p. (An alternative could be one of those plastic Ferrero Rocher chocolate boxes.) There is also a company called Marchwiel Craft Products which will be able to help you with preserving icing sugar flowers. You can call them on 01978 361518. They are specialists in encapsulating the flowers in all kinds of items such as small paperweights and door knobs.

Q

Is there a way of treating fresh flowers to put on a wedding cake?

A

Buy – or pick – the flowers as late as possible and keep them up to their necks in a bucket of water until the day before the wedding. As late in the day as possible, arrange them in soaked oasis and spray them well with water – it will have evaporated by morning. There's no need to treat or spray them with anything else; the only thing I can think of that you might spray on them is the old-fashioned egg white and sugar to crystallize them, but I think this looks really clumsy and frankly there is no need to do it. Put the arrangement onto a tiny cake board or plastic dish on top of the cake to keep the icing dry. There's a fashion at the moment for using fresh flowers pushed straight into the icing, which looks very pretty. Make sure you use edible or non-poisonous flowers, cut the stems very short and put the flowers in place at the very last moment. If you want to use a dried flower arrangement on top of the cake, a good tip is to spray them well with a non-scented hair spray before arranging them on the cake.

Jane Asher's

TOOLS

Q

Where can I buy a proper flan tin? I've looked for ages without success. I love home-made sponge flans, if only I could find something to make them in!

A

I love them too, and filled with beautifully arranged fruit they make wonderful centrepieces for parties. Divertimenti can supply a large fluted flan tin by mail order for £6.99 plus £2.95 p & p. Telephone 020 8246 4300 to order.

Q

A friend has just given me a mandolin, which I'm delighted about because I love potatoes dauphinoise, but I've got no idea how to use it without slicing my fingers off.

A

Your mandolin doesn't have to be an instrument of torture. It should have been supplied with a special finger guard, used to hold the vegetable while you slice it up and down on that fearsome blade. There should also have been clear instructions provided for its use. Maybe you're not an instruction reader: I think the world is sharply divided into those who are and those who like to toss aside the pamphlets and leaflets and plunge into new games, toy or gadgets to work things out as they go. As for me, I drive my family crazy by barking out orders on inserting part A into part X before you attempt to slot nodule C into the aperture on the back of sliding panel H and so on. If the finger guard is missing on your mandolin I think you'd be better off using a knife instead – or investing in a new gadget.

Q Two months ago I broke one of the most useful gadgets in my kitchen. It resembled a sticky-tape dispenser but was in fact a bag sealer, similar to those used in butchers' shops. I have tried everywhere to get a replacement, but without success. I know heat-sealers are available, but that's not really what I want.

A I know exactly what you mean – I used to have one, but I've been converted to the heat-sealing type (they work brilliantly and are great fun, if you're a gadget freak, as I am). Stadium Disposables can send you a bag sealer tape dispenser for £7.80 plus VAT and p & p. To order, call them on 020 8993 7686.

Q We have recently moved to a house with an electric fan-assisted oven and I am getting desperate trying to cook joints of meat and chops that aren't totally tough. I've followed the instruction book-let and reduced the temperatures but to no avail. I long for the succulent roast of my old gas cooker and I see a divorce looming if I turn out any more meat that you could sole your shoes with.

A Does your oven have a spit attachment? I had one that came with my cooker and for years I never used it until I read an article by Paul Heiney explaining that what we call roasting is really baking, and that spit roasting a joint under the intense heat of a grill is by far the best way to do it. I've never looked back. I, like you, have a fan-assisted oven and I love the way it heats up quickly and cooks stews, cakes and casseroles evenly and efficiently – but I do think the wafting air can tend to dry out uncovered meat. You may find your cooker has a 'normal' heat

Jane Asher's

setting that doesn't involve convection or a fan. Alternatively you could try cooking joints in a Pyrex covered roasting dish. The meat cooks in its own juice, and if you remove the lid for the last 15 minutes the skin crisps up nicely.

Q

All my cooking utensils are in pints and ounces, not these new metric measures which confuse many elderly people. Can you advise me where I can get a good conversion table?

A

Oh, I do so sympathize. I too get extremely confused with the imperial and metric measurements and I've been writing down recipes for years, so I should really know it all backwards by now. You may have noticed that shops are dropping the old imperial measures from their packaged food, so we'll be forced into understanding metrication very quickly. You don't need to buy anything special to enable you to convert: most cookery books have a conversion table in the front. If you do feel like investing in a simple gadget, I've always been a fan of the inexpensive Tala measuring beaker which you can use to calculate dry and liquid ingredients very easily and quickly. You can buy one from George East (Hardwares) plc, 29 High Street, West Wickham, Kent, BR4 OLP.

Q I have a very close relative who has requested a good English cookbook – a mixture of Mrs Beeton, Two Fat Ladies and Delia Smith all rolled into one. She has spent many years in America and has plenty of American and European cookery books, but nothing containing truly English recipes such as Yorkshire pudding, fairy cakes, hotpot and so on.

A No problem. I happened to be in the lovely bookshop Heffers of Cambridge recently and checked that my favourite is still available, and I'm delighted to say it is: Jane Grigson's *English Food*, published by Penguin at £6.99. A classic book by one of England's great cookery writers; I still miss her.

Q Can you recommend a good book on celebration cake decorating?

A Well now, this is obviously a subject close to my heart. I learned all my techniques and basic skills from one of the Mary Ford books – there are several available and they'll teach you all you need to know to get going. Then if it's ideas for designs you're after, a browse in the library should be inspiring. Ring my shop on 020 7584 6177 for details of a large range of mail order sugarcraft books; the website at www.sugarcraft.co.uk is also worth a visit.

Q Which kind of saucepans do you use? I swear by non-stick, but my husband says you need a heavy-bottomed pan without a non-stick surface for serious cooking.

A I think you both have good points. I'm such a lazy washer-upper that I can't bear scrubbing away at pans with scourers, so for practicality I find a non-stick surface is essential. But for really working at sauces and deglazing for gravies, etc., some of them can feel unnaturally slidy and unsatisfactory, and I had many times in the early days of non-stick when revolting black bits would appear in my soups or white sauces. I think I've found the perfect compromise in the Circulon pans (Meyer, stockists: 0151 650 6500) which have bottoms heavy enough to spread the heat evenly but without breaking your wrist, and a non-stick surface which doesn't slide about and tolerates the rough treatment I give them. (No, I know I shouldn't use metal utensils, but are you always organized enough not to grab a nearby spoon when you have to give something a quick stir?) I don't fully understand the technology, but it's apparently all to do with hi-lo ridges. If I had to choose just one pan, it would be what they call their 'paella pan', which can be used on the hob or in the oven as a roaster, stir-fryer, saucepan or casserole. Not cheap at £65, but an excellent investment for anyone who enjoys cooking.

Q My daughter is getting married and I have to prepare a buffet for 150 people. We would like to have cold salmon, but there is no way I can cook a large salmon in my oven. I have heard that it is possible to steam a salmon in a dishwasher. Could you give me any idea how to go about it?

A Yes – I'd heard of the dishwasher trick, too, but had never quite believed it. I asked my pal Orlando Murrin (the *Daily Express* Clever Cook and editor of BBC *Good Food* magazine). Apparently, the dishwasher thing is a wonderfully convincing-sounding urban myth. He has tried it just to make sure, and it makes a mess of your machine and doesn't cook the fish. It might have worked in old-fashioned machines that used more hot water, but despite trying it on a number of different cycles he's now convinced it's impossible. As is using two mobile phones (one ringing the other) to hard boil an egg, incidentally. And he's not even tempted to try frying a steak on a car cylinder like they do on *The Avengers* as he's not partial to motor oil. The solution, then, is to hire a fish kettle, either from a local fishmonger's or from a catering supplier. The catering side of HSS Hire Shops delivers nationwide and hires out large fish poachers for £6.30 plus VAT for three days. Call 0345 222000 to be put through to your nearest branch.

Jane Asher's

Q Do you keep separate wooden spoons in your kitchen, some for savoury cooking and others for sweet things? I really hate it when I'm mixing a pudding and the wooden spoon smells of last night's garlicky pasta sauce. My boyfriend thinks I'm being ridiculous when I say we should segregate them – he just uses whichever spoon is nearest.

A I hate to let the sisterhood down but I must come clean and admit that I, like your boyfriend, use whatever is nearest to hand. It's about all I can do in my chaotic kitchen to segregate the forks from the paintbrushes, let alone one type of spoon from another. I did once read some fascinating research which proved that wooden chopping boards actually eat up the bacteria and germs left on them overnight. As long as your wooden spoons are washed thoroughly there shouldn't really be a problem with old tastes and smells. Unless you would like to try setting a new trend with garlic trifle?

Q Please can you find out where I can get a baby mouli? It's a small food mill for puréeing small amounts of food for babies.

A It's such a good idea to mush up your own baby food: not only is it cheaper than buying the jars, but it means your child can get used to adult tastes and share the rest of the family's meals. We used to try to feed our babies anything I was cooking at the time – although puréeing Yorkshire pudding proved a bit of a challenge. Strictly speaking, the mouli is a hand-turned sieving device, but there are several alternatives nowadays which are easier to use. The simplest and cheapest is a Baby Food Preparation Set, which costs £6.99 and incorporates a citrus fruit squeezer, grater, strainer, masher and measurer. From JoJo, Maman, Bébé (020 7351 4112 to order). If you can spend a bit more there's a dinky little food processor – the Tomy Mini-Chef – which is just 12.5 cm high and can purée or chop food depending on the age of your child (£21.99; for your nearest stockist call 023 8066 2600). Even better is to invest in a gadget that will be useful long after your baby has grown up – an electric wand. I have a new one (Braun Hand blender, model MR 555 MCA, £44.99) that is so powerful that making mayonnaise, puréeing soups and mixing sauces is unbelievably quick and easy, and the shaft is made of stainless steel so you can use it in a hot saucepan while cooking. You get a whisk with it for cream and egg whites and – handy for you – a special chopper which would be perfect for the more rugged stage of baby foods. It really is like a magic wand – I can't imagine my kitchen without it now.

Q For my birthday my daughter gave me a Hinari juice extractor. I know that fresh fruit and vegetable juices are a very good source of vitamins (and suffering from lung cancer I need all the help I can get!), but a recipe sheet wasn't included with the juicer's instructions, so I'm a bit stuck. Can you give me a few dos and don'ts?

A What a brilliant present. I called Hinari in case they'd left out your recipe booklet by mistake, but they said they don't supply one with the machine because you can mix anything with anything to make your own concoctions. I think that's a bit feeble of them – we all need ideas to start us off with a new gadget. It's true, though, that there is almost no limit to what can be juiced: some of my favourites are apricots mixed with peach and raspberries; apple with strawberry; strawberry with peach and apricot; celery with cucumber, lettuce, spinach and parsley; carrot with pineapple and orange. You can also juice ginger by peeling the root, cutting it in slices and pushing it through your machine – if you freeze some in ice cube moulds it's very handy for adding to soups, sauces and marinades, and a teaspoon or so in some of your juice concoctions is fantastic. The only rules to remember are to wash everything well before you juice it, peel and core as necessary and add a few drops of lemon to light-coloured juices to keep them bright and fresh looking. You'll have great fun experimenting with some interesting combinations. There are several books available from the library for more ideas, or treat yourself to *Juicing for Health* by Caroline Wheater (Thorsons, £6.99), which contains lots of recipes and health-boosting information.

TROUBLESHOOTING

Q **My pastry is so hard you could build a house with it. Should I be using butter, margarine, lard, or a mixture of them all?**

A Well, I don't want to get too technical on you, but it really does depend on what you want the pastry for. The more butter you use, the richer the pastry – good for quiches and flans or when you want a buttery taste. For everyday pies, tarts and so on, I tend to use a mixture of half butter and half white cooking fat or lard – but you can easily just use entirely a proprietary vegetable shortening, which gives a very good result. Your problem with hardness is more likely to be a result of too much water, warmth and handling. Add the water very gradually, making sure the mixture doesn't become sticky, keep everything as cool as possible and handle it all to the minimum, only using a tiny bit of flour on the board and rolling pin so as not to change the proportions of your ingredients. Unlike bread dough, which needs plenty of pummeling and kneading, pastry needs very light, quick working. A good rule is: if you're feeling stressed and energetic – make bread; when you're cool and contemplative – it's pastry day.

Q **I love puff pastry but mine never seems to turn out quite right. Do you have a favourite recipe?**

A Don't bother – buy it ready made. You've obviously learned the basic principle and had a go. My attitude to pastry is similar to the way I feel about long division: it's good to know how it's done and to try it a few times, but then get a calculator. There's enormous satisfaction (and fun) in making your own puff pastry (I favour the dab and turn method) but the ready-made, either frozen or fresh, is so good now that you really needn't take the trouble unless you particularly want to.

Q **My sister bakes cakes and sponges to sell at a market and has done so for some years with great success. In the last year or so her sponges have not been as good – they seem to deflate more when cooling and have bubbles on the surface. She uses an all-in-one mixer, margarine and a supermarket's own brand of self-raising flour, and has also checked the temperature of the oven.**

A I suspect the problem may lie in the flour: the commonest cause of cakes not staying properly risen once out of the oven is either too little or (surprisingly) too much raising agent. It's possible the flour manufacturers may have changed the proportion of baking powder in their brand. Ask your sister to try using plain flour and adding baking powder according to the amounts on the tin – then at least she can experiment with using more or less until her cakes are returned to their former glory.

Q I adore tarte tatin but am never very successful with the toffee sauce. I use 2 oz castor sugar to 1 oz unsalted butter but it doesn't seem to blend well – I just get a film of melted butter around the edge. Then it seems to liquefy during cooking and gets paler: I use Granny Smith's or Cox's apples and dry them well before use. Can you tell me what I'm doing wrong?

A Much the easiest method is that recommended to me by Michel Roux many years ago:

You'll need a deep frying pan with a heat-proof handle (or a dish that can be put over direct heat) of about 10 inches' diameter. Spread the pan with 100 g (4 oz) butter, then sprinkle 200 g (8 oz) castor sugar over the base and arrange six peeled, cored and halved Cox's apples (round side down) on top. Roll out 250 g (10 oz) of puff pastry, cut a circle ¾-inch larger than the pan and tuck it over the apples. Let it rest for 30 minutes, then put the pan onto a high heat for 15–20 minutes until the butter and sugar are bubbling and have turned deep amber. Then put the pan into the oven, preheated to 425°F/220°C/Gas Mark 7, for 20 minutes, until the pastry is risen and golden, then invert it quickly onto a serving dish (do mind the hot caramel) so that the pastry is underneath and the apples on top.

This way is pretty foolproof – if you want to see step-by-step instructions you'll find the recipe in *The Roux Brothers on Patisserie*, published by Macdonald.

Jane Asher's

Q The meringue on top of my lemon meringue pie always looks good, is crisp on the outside and soft inside. But it always seems to ooze a syrup that makes the pastry soggy. Do you have a remedy for this problem?

A Meringue is so sensitive – I swear it reacts directly to my moods or my biorhythms or whatever. Sometimes mine is perfect; at other times it spreads or goes hard or weeps like yours. You can try adding all or one of the following to the mix: a pinch of corn-flour, a pinch of salt, a few drops of vinegar. And I think you may be cooking your pie a little too quickly: although you don't want the meringue to be overcooked, it sounds as if yours may need a little longer at a slightly lower temperature. Above all, don't let on if you're in a bad mood – smile broadly and you may just fool those egg whites into behaving themselves.

Q Help! Strawberry jam time is here again. How can I stop mine developing mould on top after a few months?

A I've had the same problem with strawberry jam, so I asked Orlando Murrin (the *Daily Express* Clever Cook and editor of BBC *Good Food* magazine) for advice. He says it's not our fault: in a domestic kitchen it can be difficult to keep everything as perfect-ly sterile as they do in the jam factories, and that strawberry jam is particularly prone to getting a bit mouldy after a while. So one solution is not to make too much at a time and to eat it while it's pretty fresh – certainly within 2–3 months. However, I have heard that some people leave the jars to go completely cold before covering – contrary to received wisdom – and manage to get mould-free jam; others follow the American custom of putting a layer of paraffin wax or melted candle wax on the top of each jar when it has cooled . . . and some people simply freeze the freshly made jam in the jars, then defrost and keep in the fridge to use as needed. So, one way or another, it should be possible to have jam yesterday, jam tomorrow, and . . . jam into the next millennium.

Q When I make marmalade with Seville oranges I find that, although it has set quite firm when I pour it into the jars, by the time we start to use it the marmalade has turned runny. Do you know why?

A I'm afraid there's no foolproof way. It sounds strange, but marmalade can react to humidity or a difference in air pressure. These days I cheat – I buy jam sugar. It should only be boiled for a limited time – the packet should give full instructions, but this is the only way I can guarantee success.

Q I've made Christmas puddings for many years and cannot understand why a little mould grows on some of them despite being made and stored in exactly the same way.

A I haven't had that problem and was a bit mystified, so I asked David, the sugarcraft manager at my shop, who makes the best Christmas puddings I've ever tasted and gives me one each year.

Jane Asher's

He says he always changes the greaseproof paper and foil after the initial cooking before storing and always matures them in the fridge. An interesting point he made was that sometimes, if the fruit isn't completely covered with the binding mixture, exposed fruit may start to ferment, therefore causing the mould. That is one possible explanation as to why some of yours grow mould and not others.

Q Can you tell me how to salvage my rum pot? I had been preparing it for months before Christmas, using fruits in season – strawberries, raspberries, grapes, peaches and blackcurrants steeped in white rum. But alas, when the time came it was too sweet! Can I add anything to the liquor to make it more palatable? The fruit is delicious in pavlovas but I can't bear to waste the booze.

A What a shame after all that work. How about adding a spoonful to a glass of dry white wine or champagne to make a delicious aperitif, as the French do with alcoholic syrup?

Q I enjoy the Sunday roast, but unfortunately the Yorkshire puddings always stick to the pan. As I am the one who usually lands up doing the washing up, trying to get the tray clean again, can you offer up any ideas on overcoming the problem?

A I'm a great fan of non-stick cookware when used for the right dishes – and I think this is one of them. So, the first solution is to buy a new non-stick Yorkshire pud tin. Then – whether in a new tin or your existing one – make sure you put some hot oil or fat into each space and brush it into every corner before pouring in the batter. Using the fat from around the joint is best of course, as it'll already be hot and also add to the taste of the puddings. I do it with one of those rubber baster things that look as if they're meant for performing some unpleasantly intimate medical procedure but work like a dream.

Q I love casserole dishes, but when I cook them the meat always turns out tough. What am I doing wrong?

A The main thing to remember is that meat will be more tender when it is cooked for longer on a low heat. Try turning down your gas further and giving the dishes a longer cooking time. You should also make sure that you cook them in plenty of liquid, for if the mixture becomes too dry the meat can become quite tough.

Q I recently purchased a bread-making machine and, while I am reasonably satisfied with the results, I am disappointed that the bread is not as white as I would like and does not come out tasting like shop-bought bread. I have tried different flours and altered the amount of ingredients I use (which are strong white flour, skimmed milk powder, shortening, sugar, salt, yeast and water), but my loaves are still a dull colour and texture – and not at all springy.

A I've always wanted a bread-making machine: I love the idea of flinging the ingredients in at night and waking up to the smell of home-baked bread. I'm sorry yours isn't producing the loaf you expected (although not tasting like 'shop bought' bread could be seen as an advantage). I assume your flour is bleached, as unless specified otherwise it generally is, so the dull colour that worries you may be from the skimmed milk powder (plain water will do just as well) or from your shortening. Either a white cooking fat or unsalted butter should brighten it up. But do experiment with wholemeal flours, fruit, nuts and herbs in your breads – it seems a shame to use an expensive machine just to reproduce the loaf you can buy in the corner shop.

Q **I enjoy decorating cakes and have become quite successful at piping names on them but the surface of the cake always looks bumpy, spoiling the effect. Any tips?**

A Yes, definitely! You must be using royal icing to cover your cakes, which has always seemed to me to be one of the hardest things to get right. My advice is, don't bother. Instead, cover the cake with the wonderful and easy roll-out icing which you can now buy ready-made in all sorts of colours from most supermarkets, either under their own brand name or called Regalice. Simply brush the cake with a little jam or water, roll out the icing like play-dough and smooth it over the top, trimming the edges with a sharp knife. Ring 020 7584 6177 for mail order if you can't get the colour you want.

Q I've been using roll-out icing for many years now, but my piping is a disaster. Any ideas to finish off my cakes to look a bit more professional?

A There's no question that very often the piping on a cake, particularly the writing, can let it down. There are some very handy little gadgets available that impress the words that you need onto a cake (Happy Birthday, Merry Christmas, and so on). You can then simply ice over the marks, following the shape of the letters. Cut-out decorations can also look very effective. Roll out some scraps of leftover icing, with a few drops of food colour kneaded in if you like, and cut out shapes with pastry or icing cutters. Stick them on to the cake with a little water. For cutters and writing stamps by mail order, ring the number as for the previous question.

Q When I bake a fruit cake for my family, a large crack appears in it every time. I've tried a number of different methods but nothing seems to work. What's your secret?

A I love fruit cake with a crack in the top! I know it's not the done thing, but it makes it look so different from the over-perfect, mass-produced ones, and it produces those delicious crunchy edges either side of the split. If you want to ice the cake, then you'll need to trim it with a sharp, serrated knife in any case, and you can always turn it upside down to give you an even surface for decorating. If you're determined to prevent the cracking, try one or all of the following before baking: make a definite well in the centre when you spread the mix into the tin (if you're doing

Jane Asher's

so already, make it even deeper); brush the surface with a little water and cover with a double sheet of greaseproof or baking parchment with a small hole made in the top to let out the steam. Some people put a folded tea towel (not linen) over the top. The steam inside helps seal the cracks. A little more liquid added to the mixture, such as the juice of an orange or lemon, can also help stop it cracking.

Q

What should I do about lumpy sauces? For some reason mine always go wrong when I've got people coming over.

A

To rescue lumpy sauces or curdled hollandaise you can try adding a dash of very cold liquid and then whisking like crazy. An electric hand blender is really useful here – if you have one of the newer ones with a high-powered motor it'll whizz so fast that almost every sauce can be brought together again. Or as a last resort with a lumpy sauce I've sometimes in desperation added roughly chopped herbs, capers or spring onion and pretended the lumps are all part of the general texture. No one will notice the difference.

Q I am a reasonable cook who lacks confidence, whereas my (relatively new) husband is a real natural. I have become very self-conscious about it and when I'm cooking, give a despairing commentary on what is or might be going wrong. When he occasionally comments on my collapsing pastry or whatever, I am very bad-tempered back. We share the cooking and I don't want to give it up because then I will lose confidence altogether. I'm getting so tense that supper is not at all relaxing. Any suggestions?

A Don't fight it, go with it. Ask his advice, admire his prowess: there's nothing wrong with a bit of old-fashioned hero-worship now and then – and if you are completely honest about your lack of skill it'll make him feel even cleverer. There's no unwritten rule that says women have to be natural cooks, for goodness' sake.

Q I love cooking but my boyfriend only wants to eat fish fingers and baked beans every night. He says it's a balanced meal. Is he right?

A It's certainly reasonably balanced as a meal: apart from perhaps a green vegetable, it has pretty much everything you need, but eaten every day it doesn't exactly make a balanced diet, does it? Both baked beans and fish fingers are delicious (I, like most parents, developed a very soft spot for them in the early years of child-raising) but it seems unadventurous in the extreme not to want to vary the menu a bit. And what a waste of your love of cooking! In your place I might be tempted to cook what I wanted

Jane Asher's

for tea – if he doesn't fancy Chicken Cacciatora or Toad in the Hole, he can always prepare his own exciting selection.

ENTERTAINING

Q

Friends often drop round, unannounced, at the weekend and I'd like to ensure I have enough dry ingredients that I can whip up into something tempting at a moment's notice. What should I buy in anticipation of a sociable summer?

A

Life's much easier now that shops are open all hours, but it's still a very good idea to keep a stock of dried, frozen or canned food that can be made up quickly into something interesting. Not only for guests such as your unexpected friends, but even on an evening when you can't face going out and haven't planned a meal.

Such items as dried small pasta shapes, rice, stock cubes, oils, vinegars, parmesan, tinned tomatoes and tomato purée; vacuum-packed half-baked loaves; pesto – homemade or bought, mayonnaise (to mix with tomato purée/pesto/herbs/ garlic as the base of sauces or for spreads or dips), tinned anchovies, sardines, tuna, salmon. Dried mushrooms – porcini or cepes – have a much stronger taste than fresh and after 15 minutes' soaking can be made into delicious pasta sauces and risottos or added to casseroles and onto pizzas. Red and white wine and sherry can be used to tenderize meats in marinades and to add to casseroles and sauces; long-life milk and cream taste OK when used in sauces and cooked dishes. In the freezer keep some bread (1 month); pastry (3 months); butter

Jane Asher's

(6 months); ice cream (2–3 months) and prawns (3 months). Broad beans freeze well, as do spinach and sweetcorn.

Some of my most successful meals have been created under the pressure of using what's in the cupboard or freezer – you'll be surprised just how much you can make of it. If in doubt, gently cook an interesting selection of leftovers in a little oil in a saucepan, add some stock and simmer for 10 minutes or so and purée with a hand blender. Add a few chopped herbs and a swirl of cream and call it 'soupe surprise'. Perfection.

Q **This will be our last big family Christmas get-together in my sister's house before they move to a smaller property. There are 25 of us, and in order to ease the catering strain on her we have agreed to divide up the days between families, each taking all the necessary food for lunch and dinner. My 'day' is the day after Boxing Day I will be travelling 200 miles on Christmas Eve and plan to cook and freeze the food in advance. Please could you help me to devise a balanced menu? I have trawled through all my cookery books but I seem to have taken all the likely dishes on previous years. A small amount of preparation and cooking in situ is possible, but the kitchen is very small. The only other proviso is that I do not eat beef.**

A It's such a good idea to divide up all the work. We do the same for the meal on Christmas Day in my house. My mother brings her great brandy butter, my sister's mother-in-law brings her unbeatable mince pies, my brother-in-law the wine, my sister the cranberry sauce and so on. I'm hoping to end up with nothing left to do. As 'your' day is the one after Boxing Day I'd be inclined to avoid meat altogether: everyone will have had their fill of turkey and, as you don't eat beef, it'll suit you perfectly. How about a home-made thick vegetable soup for lunch, with crusty bread and cheese? Cut the vegetables in large chunks and include some sweet potatoes and red peppers to make it a little different and add some red wine, soy sauce and a pinch of sugar to the stock to give it richness and flavour. For supper, I suggest a fish pie, again making it a little sophisticated by adding just a few scallops, prawns and salmon to the usual haddock or cod and adding cream and tarragon to the sauce instead of just milk and parsley. Decorate the mashed potato topping with some prawns in their shells and it'll look as good as it tastes. Everything will freeze perfectly and give you almost nothing to do on the day except reheat it all and perhaps make a green salad. Follow with an interesting selection of fresh fruit (which will contrast nicely with the rich puddings of the previous days), and you can't go wrong.

Q **Have you got any time-saving tips for preparing the Christmas meal?**

A

How about these:

- Serve a simple starter – consommé is traditional but many people prefer a lighter appetizer such as melon with avocado in a mint dressing.

- If you're eating at midday the turkey can be cooked overnight in a low oven (250°F/120°C/Gas Mark ½). To keep the breast moist, cook breast-side down until the last 40 minutes, then turn over to brown.

- Cook bacon rolls and sausages in the oven to save watching the grill.

- Make the bread sauce the day before to allow the flavours to combine.

- Green vegetables can be cooked in advance until al dente. Refresh immediately under cold running water to retain their colour, then heat through in boiling water for one minute at the last moment.

- For roast potatoes, parboil them first and then make sure you coat them with very hot fat from around the turkey. They will need to cook for an hour altogether – turn the oven up to a very high temperature (400°F/ 200°C/Gas Mark 6) for the last 30 minutes, as they lose their crunchiness if kept in a low oven too long.

Q This year I am 'doing' Christmas at my house, and I am getting increasingly anxious about the day. How can I take the stress out of entertaining and even (perish the thought!) enjoy it myself? I am expecting several children to come.

A You should be able to relax and enjoy Christmas, but in reality it does mean gathering together people with whom you might not otherwise choose to spend your time, and there's no denying that this can be stressful – not to mention all the cooking involved. The best advice is not to aim for perfection, because it will make you and everyone around you miserable. Try and do as much in advance as possible (see above). Make sure the house is warm when people arrive – you may be hot from cooking and not aware of it being a bit chilly. Have drinks ready to offer them straight away, including soft drinks for children or drivers. Put lots of candles about the place to make it feel festive and give a beautiful, flattering glow, but be extra mindful of safety as there will be children around. Play a CD or cassette of carols quietly in the background to get the atmosphere right and the day off to a good start. Traditional games such as charades can be a great way to channel the energy of over-excited children, but it's best not to force everyone to play as some people simply hate them. If they want to slump in front of the telly watching James Bond, that's fine. Oh, and leave the washing up until Boxing Day.

Jane Asher's

Q I am planning a Thanksgiving party to raise money for the Sight Savers charity. On previous occasions when catering for a large number I have served a cold meal, but this time I would like to do something different. How can I serve hot turkey to about 50 people and keep it hot – because I know you should never reheat poultry?

A I'm sure your party guests will be delighted to be served hot food: at this time of year a cold buffet just doesn't seem so welcoming. The dangers of re-heating poultry arise when it is not completely cooked through the first time, and, even when it is, it's important that when it's heated the second time it must be piping hot all the way through. If you follow these two rules there is no problem: many delicious dishes are made from pre-cooked chicken or turkey (coping with Christmas leftovers would be impossible if not). How about cooking two or three large turkeys, cutting the meat into bite-sized portions and mixing it into a white sauce with some mushrooms, cooked sliced onions and chopped herbs? Turn it into some attractive oven-to-table dishes and then you can either simply top it with some browned bread-crumbs and call it fricassee, or with some ready-made puff pastry and call it a pie. Keep it chilled until needed, then put into a moderate oven until hot right through and the pastry has risen and turned golden brown.

Q My sister and I are 12 and 14 years old and are planning a special birthday picnic for our mum, who turns 40 in a few weeks' time. Apart from sandwiches, have you any other ideas for nice food?

A What a wonderful treat for your mum! If you want to be able to eat everything with your fingers, then stuffed pitta bread makes a good change from sandwiches, and you can choose some fillings that you know she likes and are a bit special. A small packet of smoked salmon, for example, can go a long way if you use it with cream cheese, or try fresh crab mixed with some mayonnaise and raw sliced mushrooms. You can also hollow out vegetables like courgettes (split lengthways) or small peppers (tops sliced off) and fill them with bought fish paté or hummus or egg mayonnaise. Crusty wholemeal rolls make good food containers too – cut the tops off, take out the crumbs and brush inside and out with melted butter, then crisp them in the oven for 5 minutes before filling with something like tinned ratatouille sprinkled with parmesan. Put the tops back on after filling them. Chicken drumsticks are good too and easy to eat – bake them for 50–60 minutes at 400°F/200°C/Gas Mark 6. To make them a bit more fancy you can slash the tops and paint them with some lemon juice and sprinkle some mixed herbs over them before cooking. (Please be careful with sharp knives and the hot oven though, won't you?)

Let everything get cold and wrap it all in foil to transport it. Take plenty of cos lettuce leaves and some salad cream, a punnet of

Jane Asher's

strawberries and a jar of sugar to dip them in and you'll have the perfect English picnic. Also, you might want to organize something cold and delicious to drink.

Q We are having our baby christened soon and would like to entertain around 40 adults and 10 young children to tea in the garden. It would need to be prepared and set out in advance as we will all get back from the church at the same time. I'd like it to be pure finger food (no spreading or eating with forks involved) and I'd like to avoid hot food. I've got as far as cucumber sandwiches and cocktail sausages, but have you any more interesting suggestions? I'm also worried about having to make hundreds of cups of tea – should I just fill thermoses with water and get the guests to make it themselves?

A Little filo pastry triangles are easy to make and look very pretty: Use ready-made filo fresh or frozen and defrosted. Take one sheet and brush it with light olive oil (melted butter is traditional but is fattier and more greasy) then cut it into four long strips.

Lay a small teaspoon of filling in one corner of a strip and fold it over to make a triangle. Fold the strip over and over again, each time making a triangle and brushing with more oil as you go, then stick down the end and put it on a baking sheet.

Make as many as you need, then bake them for 15–20 minutes at 350°F/180°C/Gas Mark 4) until golden brown.

There are all sorts of fillings you could try, but my favourite is cooked, drained spinach processed and mixed with seasoned cream cheese. And spiral sandwiches are that bit special:

Cut a loaf in slices lengthways, trim off the crusts, spread with filling and roll up carefully. Cut each roll into 1-inch thick pieces. Use fillings like smoked salmon, crab and mayonnaise, chopped egg with capers or cooked chicken chopped into mayonnaise with a pinch of curry powder.

Baby meringues are cute (maybe tinted pale pink or blue as appropriate?), and home-made Vienna biscuits dipped in chocolate look great and taste wonderful.

The plan to get the guests to make their own tea is excellent, but the thermos idea doesn't sound very celebratory: how about hiring a large urn for your hot water? If you think of it as a Russian samovar it sounds quite romantic. The catering side of HSS Hire Shops delivers nationwide. Call 0345 222000 to be put through to your nearest branch – tell them it's for a party and they may have a glamorous-looking one. Don't forget the cake!

Q I'm having a cocktail party and wonder if you have any suggestions for canapés that I can make in advance? I don't want to be fiddling around at the last minute.

A These recipe ideas are easy, yet give impressive results.

For smoked salmon spirals, spread soft goat's cheese on to slices of smoked salmon, roll up and wrap in cling film. Freeze for up to one month, then thaw in the fridge and cut into slices to serve. Buy some ready-to-bake croissant dough, cut it into small

Jane Asher's

pieces and wrap a tasty filling in each one before baking – Gruyère cheese and mango chutney, paté and cranberry sauce or sausage and mustard are great combinations. Freeze before or after baking (after, if the dough was bought frozen) and use within two months, reheating or cooking as necessary.

Q **I am planning a devastatingly romantic meal for the man in my life and am desperate for it to be a success. He's not a fan of puddings, and cheese gives me a migraine, so how can I round if off in appropriately grand style?**

A You can find luscious tropical fruits in many shops now. Mango, paw-paw, kiwi and, of course, passion fruit all look and taste very sexy. Cut them into pieces to eat with your fingers (and the passion fruit in half to scoop out with a teaspoon) and put them on a dish to share, with some lime quarters to squeeze over. Your fingers will get very sticky and need sucking and the juices will dribble down your chins in the candlelight. Follow with a luscious liqueur coffee. To make Gaelic coffee, lace a glass of freshly brewed coffee with one measure of Scotch whisky and add sugar to taste. Stir it fast until the brew is really swirling, then trickle in some double cream over the back of a spoon. The layer of cream should remain on top of the coffee and the man of your dreams should be well impressed.

Q I went out to buy a new dining room table and ran into a friend who said I should buy a round one because it's good feng shui. My existing one is square – which might explain why my dinner parties are often such a disaster. Is there anything in this?

A I tend to cringe whenever feng shui is mentioned: I can't help bracketing it with things like horoscopes on my mental list of irritating nonsense. But there's no doubt that some shapes and colours are more aesthetically pleasing than others and influence one's mood. On your behalf I've buried my rationalism for a while and studied the *Feng Shui House Book* by Gina Lazenby (Conran Octopus, £20) which had some interesting things to say about tables. Apparently, circles hold creative energy and are life-enhancing, which makes round tables more comfortable for informal gatherings such as dinner parties. Square or rectangular tables are more suitable for discussing practical issues (obviously no one told King Arthur). But I find the problem with round tables is the size – if you want to entertain more than six people, the distance across the middle can stretch too far for comfort and make conversation very difficult. We used to have a large, old, rectangular dining table which tended to feel a bit severe, so last year we invested in a new one which is oval – how's that for compromise? So far I love it, and if the creative energy is slipping off the straight sides, then luckily the family is usually too busy eating to notice.

Jane Asher's

Q I never seem to be able to create those gorgeous-looking table displays you see in magazines. Do you have any foolproof ideas for a glamorous (but cheap) centrepiece?

A For stunning table centrepieces, forget crystal vases and expensive flowers, we're talking cheap, cheerful and eye-catching here. The following ideas will make real impact when your guests enter the dining room.

For a fruit pyramid: carve a cone shape out of florist's foam and place on a stemmed dish. Slice 5 cm from the top and replace with a pineapple top. Use cocktail sticks or florist's wire to attach satsumas, greengages, Chinese gooseberries and halved kiwi fruit to the cone, spiralling them in bands around the display. Fill in any gaps with ivy leaves.

For a candlelit tray: take an ornamental mirror, a silver tray or even a chopping board covered in silver foil and group six candles of various heights and widths at one end. Surround the tray with some sprays of foliage – yew, ivy and snowberries look really pretty. When lit, the candlelight will be reflected in the surface – it looks enchanting.

Q I have agreed to be chief cook and bottle-washer for around 20 children plus adult chaperones at a youth hostel in Cornwall while they do their week on theatre tour. I've never done it before, and would be grateful for any suggestions for basic food that can be made with the help of gas rings, grill and microwave. Breakfast will be the usual Cornflakes, toast and tea; then I have to dish up an evening meal at around 11 p.m. and would prefer not to serve up beans on toast every time. Any suggestions would be gratefully received.

A What a heroine you are! Not only feeding them all when they come back at night, but having to listen to all that self-indulgent chat that we actors inevitably indulge in after the show ('Darling, you were wonderful,' etc.). The quicker you can get them all eating the better, and the priorities will be quantity and economy, as I assume you'll be on a pretty tight budget. If they're not provided, I should hire a couple of very large stew pans so you can cook big casseroles, soups and pastas on the gas rings – these can be filling and economical, and very cheering late in the evening. They also have the great advantage of not having to be timed to the minute. The catering side of HSS Hire Shops delivers nationwide – call 0345 222000 to be put through to your nearest branch. (And why not use the pans to make delicious, healthy porridge for a couple of breakfasts as a break from all that toasting?) Try things like a simple leek, onion and potato soup served with hunks of bread and cheese; a rich Minestrone with plenty of cannellini beans (cheapest bought dried, then

Jane Asher's

soaked and cooked); a lentil soup with added tomatoes, onions and broken-up spaghetti; macaroni with a cheese sauce. An Irish stew is always a good bet – this is my favourite:

Peel and slice (half-inch thick) 6 medium potatoes and put half of the slices in the bottom of the stew pan.

Peel and slice (quarter-inch thick) 4 large onions and add half of them to the pan.

Add 1½ kg (3 lb) boneless neck or shoulder of lamb, cut roughly into chunks and season with salt, pepper and ¼ tsp dried thyme. Cover with the rest of the onions and, finally, the potatoes. Pour in just enough cold water to cover, bring to the boil then simmer for about 1½ hours.

Serve with some chopped fresh herbs sprinkled over, and crusty bread on the side. This will serve six to eight people, so, for you, three times the quantity should keep your young actors and chaperones well nourished.

Q I have been nominated by my sixth-form college to organize a fancy dress ball, and wonder if you can use your theatrical know-how to dream up a theme. We'd like it to give people plenty of scope for imagination, but don't want them to have to go out and spend a fortune hiring costumes.

A Very thoughtful of you – it's the fancy dress invitations that specify 'The Court of Louis XIV in August 1648' and such like that fill one with horror. Choose something that allows not only for small budgets, but also for those who hate dressing up (witty gestures can be useful for those that do: a drinking straw in the top pocket to be 'The Last Straw'; a stamp stuck on a lapel for 'First Class Mail' and so on). It's not only the money that makes hiring costumes unsatisfactory; it's far more fun when guests use their imagination and concoct something themselves – and it certainly needn't be expensive: my brother-in-law once flung a scarf round his neck with an old tyre attached to the end and went as Isadora Duncan. You could offer something like Zodiac (interesting to see who turns up as Virgo); Stone Age (plenty of scope for saucy minimalism with a bit of fake fur) or make it a wider category like 'Comedy' or 'Glamour'. If you want it to be a more traditional ball then you could specify fancy dress for masks or headdresses only: that way your guests can wear black tie and long dresses and simply let their imagination go to their heads.

Q I have just moved into my new flat – the first ever place that I have bought. I promised my work team I would have them round for dinner as soon I moved in, but the only problem is I don't yet have a dining table, or indeed many chairs. How can I improvise with cushions and a small coffee table? And what on earth can I cook for six hungry young advertising executives? I only have one electric ring.

A This is the perfect opportunity to go Moroccan. Scatter your cushions in a circle around the coffee table, put some good music on the CD and pass round some cold beers as soon as your guests arrive. Serve them Chicken Tagine, which is very

Jane Asher's

easy, filling and delicious (I cooked it twice last week!):

Buy two large chickens and cut them up into serving pieces. Put them into a large, heavy-bottomed saucepan with a tight-fitting lid. Peel two onions, slice them into rings and add to the chicken with 75 g (3 oz) butter. Pour in just enough water to cover the chicken, bring to the boil, then cover the pan and let it simmer gently for about 30 minutes.

Add two more chopped onions, 1½ tsp saffron powder, 1 tsp ground ginger, 1 rounded tbsp paprika, [fr1/2] tsp ground cinnamon, 150 g (6 oz) pitted dates and 350 g (14 oz) thawed frozen broad beans. Stir well, cover the pan and simmer for another 30 minutes. Season to taste and sprinkle with chopped coriander and parsley.

Serve with couscous (I'm assuming you have a kettle!): make some chicken stock with a cube and 725 ml (1¼ pts) boiling water, then pour it over 450 g (1 lb) couscous in a bowl. Cover and leave for 5 minutes until the liquid is absorbed.

I'd suggest you serve the meal in bowls with plenty of paper napkins around so they can finish off the chicken with their fingers. Offer a green salad to follow, which can be eaten in the same bowls – the meat juices left over will make it taste even better. Then just let them help themselves from a selection of fruit.

This recipe comes from a great new book of chicken recipes that can all be cooked on top of the stove, so it might be worth your getting it. *Pan-cooked Chicken Dishes* (£5.99) is part of the series *Recipes from Around the World* published by IMP and only available by mail order: ring 020 7258 2628 for details.

Q We're having a family celebration and have to seat 12 people when our table holds only 6. There's an old trestle table we can use but we don't have a cloth large enough and it's not worth buying one just for the occasion. How can we disguise it and make it look special?

A This is really easy. Drape a white double sheet right over the table so that it reaches down to the floor on all sides, making a pleat in the middle if it's too big. If you can't get the length just right, don't panic: fold the bottom edges under in a rather trendy, bunched-up look. Use two singles if you haven't a double and simply pin or tack them together along the top of the table. Then take a coloured table cloth or even a single sheet in a pretty blue if you've got one – and put it over the white one. If you want to dress it up even more, pull up the over-cloth every 40 cm or so to make large swags, and pin them in position. Decorate the apex of each swag with a small bunch of flowers or leaves. You could even use little muslin bags of sugared almonds or silver dragees for a wedding or anniversary, and you can add lengths of small ivy leaves along the top edges of the table. Keep everything in place with dress-makers' pins, unless there are young children around, in which case it's safer to stitch them in position or use safety pins. Make sure you pick a clean, ironed sheet and that any holes or mends will be hidden under the top one. A steamer can be brilliant for getting out any creases once it's in position, but they cost the earth. You could hire one if you're giving a huge do and want all the curtains, upholstery, table cloths and clothes looking really smart: they seem to take the wrinkles out of everything (excluding faces, unfortunately), or you can buy little hand-held ones which work pretty well.

Q In your book *Easy Entertaining*, you mention cocktail sparklers, but I can't seem to find them in my local shops. Where can I buy them to jazz up my drinks?

A The name 'cocktail' is very misleading – they are really just indoor sparklers which I used in that book to brighten up a Baked Alaska; I wouldn't recommend them for drinks. The theory is that they don't shed as many bits of ash as the outdoor ones, but you must obviously still treat them with respect.

Q As an alternative to accompanying my children (aged 10 and 12) on the usual gruesome rounds of Trick or Treat, I rashly promised that they could invite friends round for a Hallowe'en party. Now I'm regretting it – I can't think how to entertain a dozen excited kids for the evening. Any ideas?

A You can't beat good old apple-bobbing and coin-in-flour for messy fun, but my children's favourite was the following spooky game.

Someone dresses up as a witch (a simple long black coat and

some sort of cheap hat will do, as none of it will be clearly seen). The witch sits in an almost completely dark room and tells the guests, sitting in a circle, how much she likes to eat little children for supper (cue squeals of horrified delight). 'Would you like to feel some of my favourite pieces?' she asks, and passes round bits of 'body' for the children to feel (cue even louder squeals). Peeled grapes make good eyes, pieces of damp chamois leather or similar for skin, wet sponge for brain, raw sausages for fingers, cooked spaghetti for veins and arteries, warm milk for blood, and so on. You must obviously suit the spookiness of the story to the ages you are entertaining, and if necessary little ones can sit on adults' laps, but it always goes down well. My parents used to play it with us as children, and once my doctor father brought home a skeleton from the hospital, sat it at the head of the table and wired it up to speak to us.

Q I owe a glamorous couple several meals and have finally bitten the bullet and invited them to dinner in two weeks' time. I am the world's worst – and most neurotic – cook. Could you suggest an impressive yet simple menu to make sure the evening is a success? They are both vegetarian.

A How irritating of them to be both glamorous and vegetarian: it's unlikely they'll be content with wholemeal bread and lentils. Never mind – as someone who was terrified of giving dinner parties when I was first married I have built quite a portfolio of foolproof but interesting dishes. The most important thing is to

Jane Asher's

choose at least two courses that can be prepared ahead. If you've never cooked them before, try them out on a partner or friend first. On the day, get the table laid and the room tidied early. The less you have to worry about in the evening, the less you'll panic about the food. Don't try to be too ambitious: there are plenty of simple meals that can be glamorous without your needing to spend the evening jumping up and down every few minutes to check on how the next course is going in the kitchen.

For a starter you can't beat marinated brie; it looks and tastes fabulous and couldn't be easier. Gently heat some sliced garlic, dried basil and black peppercorns in olive oil for a few moments until the oil bubbles (don't burn the garlic). Then, after letting it cool a little, pour it over some thinly-sliced ripe brie in a shallow dish. Leave it for at least 4 hours (in the fridge you can keep it up to two days, but bring it out 2–4 hours before it is needed). Serve two or three slices for each person with some lamb's lettuce, and at the last minute dribble a little of the marinade over the cheese and leaves.

For a main course, blanch a selection of vegetables such as carrots, mangetout and green beans and layer them in a glass dish with sliced Spanish tomatoes, seasoning each layer. Rub together some breadcrumbs, cheddar cheese, flour and butter into a crumble mixture and sprinkle it over the vegetables. Store it in the fridge until you're ready to cook it. Then place in the oven for about an hour until the top is golden brown, and serve with tomato sauce (as you're feeling a bit nervous why not cheat on this and buy one of the many excellent ready-made tomato pasta sauces available?). The sides of the crumble can look beautiful through the glass if you layer the colours alternately.

For dessert, look around the supermarket for the best soft fruit and buy a little more than you'll need so you can pile it generously in a pretty dish. Sprinkle a little chopped fresh mint over it and serve with marscarpone instead of cream to make it a bit more special.

Q I would like to have a family gathering of my cousins, aunts and uncles without their myriad young children. I live in a small cottage without space for lots of children tearing around and I would like to have the chance to have a civilized adult catch-up with everyone. How canI organize a gathering without offending anyone?

A I'm sure they will understand. As long as you make it absolutely clear that no one's child is being invited and that it is not just their particular little darlings you cannot bear to have around, then there should be no problem. Do give them plenty of warning, though: arranging baby-sitting can be time-consuming. Maybe some of them live near each other and can organize their children to get together in a family crèche. Also, it would be thoughtful to ring to ask whether lunch or dinner would be easier for them to get to without offspring. I suspect that the daytime would be a better bet for most of them. I should think that they

Jane Asher's

will all enjoy the chance to have a peaceful family get-together just as much as you will.

Q **I have, perhaps rather foolishly, offered to look after my sister's young brood (aged 18 months and 3 years) for two days. I do not have children myself and could do with some tips on how to amuse them: I'd rather not go out and buy any expensive toys.**

A At about 18 months onwards handbags become fascinating to babies: it's worth finding an old one and filling it with a good selection of bits and pieces to be turned out and examined: old keys on a ring; scrumpled paper; a teaspoon; a rattle and so on, remembering to watch for anything sharp or swallowable, and never leaving the baby alone with it. It'll never be quite as interesting as the real thing, but may while away a few minutes. Spoons and saucepans can be banged about and enjoyed; water in a washing up bowl put on the floor on a large plastic sheet with a plastic cup or two; play dough and plastic cutters – even a garlic press for the older child. Some simple baking always goes down well – not just the usual buns or jam tarts, but recipes like home-made pizzas or bread: new one-stage dried yeast makes it very easy. A wonderfully simple game for very young toddlers is to sit on the floor and tear up bits of newspaper, then throw them up in the air and make snow-storms. If things get fractious the best course of action is to quickly get out of the house: a trip in the buggy can be a happy distraction in itself; or there may be a particular interest that can be indulged: a visit to the bus station, to the zoo, to the nearest building site to peep through the viewing holes in the fence, to a friend with children of the same age.

TABLE MANNERS

Q I was having dinner with a very 'proper' friend when she began talking about the correct way to eat a bread roll. I think she was hinting that I was wrong to cut it in half, butter each side and then take bites. Do you have any idea who's right and whether this is important in terms of etiquette?

A It depends on what one means by 'important'. To me the fact that your 'proper' friend hinted that you were eating your roll in the 'wrong' way was the height of bad manners, and far outweighs any rules of etiquette. At my rather 'proper' school they did indeed teach me that bread should be broken into small pieces which are buttered individually, so if you mind about being correct then I have to concede that your friend was right. It's a bit like worrying about which side to serve food from (apparently we should serve from the right and remove from the left) – but I can't help thinking that courtesy is far more important than these 'rules'.

Q Could you please sort out a disagreement between me and my husband? Which is the correct way to leave a knife and fork when you have finished your meal? Together, straight in front of you, or slightly to the side? And also, what is the correct way to eat soup?

A The knife and fork question is easy: definitely together straight in front of you. Americans tend to leave them splayed about, which I find very confusing: you're never quite sure if they've finished or not. The soup question I had to check, and there are varying opinions, but Debrett's states that you should dip the far edge of your spoon into the soup, and tip the soup (quietly!) into your mouth from the front edge of the spoon. To finish up the last of the soup, tilt the bowl away from you. To be really 'correct' you shouldn't use one of the relatively recent round soup spoons at all but a tablespoon, but I think that's taking things too far – I'm not chucking out all my soup spoons for anyone. When the Queen comes to dinner I'm sure she'll understand.

Jane Asher's

SOCIAL OCCASIONS

Q We will be celebrating our diamond wedding anniversary this year. We have heard that if we advise the Queen, she will send her good wishes. What is the correct procedure for this?

A The monarchy has been marking this sort of occasion since 1917, and last year the Queen sent about 9,000 messages of congratulation to couples celebrating their diamond wedding anniversary. But you're right: brilliant and perceptive as Her Majesty is, she just might not remember it's your diamond wedding unless you tip her the wink. Put your request in writing, well in advance, to the Assistant Private Secretary to the Queen, Buckingham Palace, London SW1A 1AA, marking your envelope 'Anniversaries' in the top left-hand corner. Enclose your name and address and a photocopy of an official document such as a marriage certificate that gives the date on which the wedding took place.

Q My husband and I have to attend one of his work functions next month – it's a celebratory millennium dinner and awards ceremony. The thing is that I haven't been to a 'do' like this for ages – the last time was back in the seventies when everyone wore long dresses. My daughter now informs me (as only teenagers can) that 'No one wears long frocks any more, silly,' which worries me somewhat as my only posh dress is a rather glam green long

taffeta number. Could I get away with it or should I go out and buy a cocktail dress?

A You're not the only person who hasn't been to a do like this for ages – it must be at least a thousand years since anyone has, so a precedent has yet to be set on correct celebratory Millennium wear. Your daughter is wrong on this one anyway: long dresses are frequently worn nowadays (*and* seventies' styles are now popular again), and at the last couple of awards ceremonies I went to they were in the majority (and I'm not just talking show-biz: the most recent ones were for the Pipeline Industries Guild). As someone who dresses up for a living I still love it and, as long as I know I won't be horribly overdressed, I wear long on any excuse. Your green taffeta sounds divine: wear it and knock 'em dead.

Q **When a man you have recently met insists he loves cooking and invites you to his place for dinner, does he always really only have prandial enjoyment on his mind?**

A If he really does enjoy cooking and is any good at it, he's still a relatively rare member of the species and is therefore worth cultivating. Enjoy the meal. If he doesn't and you suspect it's the modern equivalent of asking you up to see his etchings, then the decision must be yours: are his other attributes tempting enough to overcome the lack of boeuf bourguignon? Have a good exit line and an escape route ready in case you're unsure.

Q A young woman among the guests I have invited to stay with me for the weekend is in her twenties with a marked exhibitionist streak. She wears extremely revealing clothes and leaves the door of the bathroom open when she's bathing – which might alarm older members of the party, to say nothing of myself. How can I prevent her from, for example, sunbathing topless as she has done in the past, without offending her or her husband, who is much older than his wife and proud of her body? He is an old friend of mine and I do not wish to upset him.

A You're kidding! Firstly, the chances of the sun being hot enough to sunbathe are minimal, and secondly if it does and she's in her twenties and not unattractive then you'll become the most popular hostess around. As it's difficult to open a newspaper or turn on the television without being confronted by naked breasts, it's hard to believe anyone can still be seriously alarmed by them on a sun-lounger. Now if you're talking school fêtes, that's a different matter.

Q My daughter is getting married next year and I am already worrying about whom I should tip and how much. Our hairdresser will charge £25 for the bride's cut and blow dry on the morning of the wedding. How much extra should I give him? (I tend to leave £1 on a normal visit.) Then there's the vintage Ford car and Rolls Royce – how much do I tip the drivers? Finally the reception; this is costing over £2,000 – if we give an extra 10% here, as we usually do when we go out for a meal, £200

seems rather a lot. What do you think? We want to do this right.

A Don't worry: I've asked around and there seem to be so many variants on the amounts people tip (if at all) in this situation that there's no question of 'doing it right' – it's entirely up to individual choice. Car companies tell me that sometimes a gratuity is included in the price of car hire; sometimes the bride's father passes the driver £20 or so – the generosity depending somewhat on the amount of champagne consumed – others suggest anything from 10–20%. In other words, there seem to be no strict rules – the bride's parents can reward good service to whatever degree they see fit. Unless you get particularly spectacular service you don't need to add 10% to the price of the reception: some managers told me they often don't get anything extra at all. Perhaps £50 or so if you're pleased would be suitable? And why not give the hairdresser a rise of 100% in his tip – an extra pound will hardly figure in the great scheme of things. Overall I suggest you set aside the maximum you can afford and then forget about it: there are far more enjoyable things to worry about in the lead-up to the great day.

Q **My daughter's wedding is in eight months' time, and I have paid one-third of the cost of the reception as a deposit. I would like to know what is the current practice regarding who pays for what. We do not know my future son-in-law's parents well, having met them only fleetingly two years ago, and they have made no approach to us so**

Jane Asher's

far about the wedding. **My wife says that if we approach them now it will look as if it is just an attempt to get them to contribute, but I feel we should meet some time before the wedding. I don't wish to appear mercenary, but in view of the fact that there are more than 200 guests, I think we need to know what it will cost us overall. What should I do?**

'Current practice' is a good phrase, as there's no doubt it varies from what one might call 'correct etiquette', which I believe still dictates that the bride's family pays for the wedding in its entirety. Nowadays it's very common for both sides to contribute, but I think you might feel embarrassed if you asked directly. I would have thought an invitation to a meal at your house would be taken as a friendly gesture, rather than an approach for funding. Once chatting, you can soon drop a few hints about future preparations.

WHERE CAN I FIND ...?

Everything can be found somewhere if you keep looking long and hard enough – you need to think of yourself as a detective trying to unearth the clues that will ultimately lead you onto the right track. Start by checking the most obvious places: your local telephone book, Directory Enquiries or the Yellow Pages (don't forget Talking Pages for numbers out of your area), and if the first people you call can't help, ask them if they know someone who can. Don't be put off if your first leads come to nothing; keep trying and you'll unearth someone who will let you tap into their network of contacts and help you to get closer and closer to the information you need.

Use your local library and, as well as trying their reference books, magazines and computer databases, ask them for the numbers of umbrella organizations such as the National Association of Whatever-it-is, or the British Thingummy Club – inspired guesses as to what these official bodies are called prove right more often than you'd imagine. There are organizations or societies for almost every type of interest you can imagine, and they exist purely in order to help people just like you. Once you find one that's relevant, ring them and pick the brains of an expert in the field – be keen and enthusiastic and you'll soon get help to take you on to the next stage.

Scan adverts in newspapers and magazines, talk to friends and family who are in the business. Use the phone rather than wasting time going from place to place on the off-chance that you'll come across what you're looking for – these days it's possible to find and pay for most things without leaving the house. If you have access to a computer, the Internet can be particularly helpful: web pages are springing up to cover a vast cross-section of subjects, and there isn't much you can't find out about if you learn to use the search engines efficiently or have a friend who can do it for you.

If you're looking for a particular product, call a department store and ask to speak to a buyer in that department; if you've got a problem or a question about a product or a service, ferret out the company's phone number from the instruction manual or from whoever supplied you with the item, and call their customer services team. Once you get through to the right people, you'll find that companies are all more than willing to help you out – many have banks of people on the end of a phone just waiting for you to call and ask their advice.

Above all, keep trying. Don't be put off. Remember that everything is out there somewhere!

HOUSEHOLD ITEMS

Q After months of doing up our house, we are finally getting round to our bedroom. I would like to replace our old second-hand bed, but read recently that orthopaedic mattresses are not actually that good for you. What would you recommend? I would like to buy an iron bedstead but have a proper solid mattress with it.

A I think you should talk to the Sleep Council (yes, it really exists and must be a great place to work: if you're late you can just say you slept in and they probably nod approvingly). They can provide you with all sorts of information about what to look for when buying both beds and mattresses. Their spokesperson says there is not really any such thing as an orthopaedic mattress – it's just a marketing term. Having said that, the sort of mattress and base you buy will make a huge difference to the quality of sleep you get and to the support you provide for your back, and everyone's needs are different. The Sleep Council's *Bed Buyer's Guide* will tell you everything you need to know – for a copy send an SAE to them at High Corn Mill, Chapel Hill, Skipton, North Yorkshire BD23 1NL. Incidentally, if you have already found an antique bedstead you like and want a mattress and base made to fit, the Odd Mattress Factory supplies them in any shape or size and in various degrees of squashiness – call 01772 786666.

Q I am trying to replace the crystal stoppers of an Edwardian cruet. Could you suggest anyone who deals in them? Or do you know a glass grinder who could grind down the ones I have purchased but are too big to fit into the necks of the bottles?

A A glass company called Blue Crystal tell me it would be far better to start from scratch and buy the right size: they make new stoppers to fit any bottle and can match them to the style of the original in whatever shape you'd like, either in cut glass or a plainer design. An uncut round glass stopper would probably cost less than £15. Ring them on 020 7278 0142 for details. Now, of course, you'll have to find bottles to fit the over-large stoppers you bought. This could go on for some time . . .

Q I would like to hang coloured, patterned voile in all my windows, but while I have looked everywhere for this sort of fabric, there seems to be very little choice. Do you know anywhere that has a good selection?

A Your house sounds like it's going to be the model of modern chic – all floaty and airy, even if everyone ends up waking at dawn! Try a company called Malabar, who tell me they have around 20 different designs such as checks, stripes and an appliqué effect in 100 or so colourways. Prices range from approximately £9 to £30 per metre. For details of your local stockists, call 020 7501 4200.

Q Can you recommend a supplier of well-made teapots? I have one from which the handle has come unstuck, and my spare one is a bad pourer.

A Pristine Pottery, on 01782 329931 make teapots that are all moulded in one piece, so no embarrassing moments with leaky teapots when the vicar comes to tea.

Q This seems like a silly question, but it concerns a small item that would make a big difference to my life. I'm looking for a tea caddy spoon and have no idea where to find one.

A Try telephoning Whittard of Chelsea (020 7924 1888) who supply long-forgotten but essential items such as these. They have a mail order service.

Q Some time ago I broke the glass funnel of an oil lamp. I heard that there's a shop in London that can obtain them – do you know which one?

A A large selection of new oil lamp chimneys is available from Christopher Wray Lighting: prices range from £1.75 to £19.50. Call 020 7736 8434 for branches nationwide or 020 7384 2888 for mail order. The firm also offers a restoration service. It's important to get a funnel that's the right shape as well as size, or your lamp won't work efficiently. Another useful contact for antique funnels is David Turner Antiques and Restoration, which always has a selection. Call 020 7249 2379 for more details.

Q I am moving to a cottage in Norfolk and have searched in vain for a single-sized (i.e. 3-foot) four-poster bed. I know they exist – can you help me locate one please?

A Single four-posters certainly do exist, though they seem to be at something of a premium. You could try A Barn Full of Brass Beds who are based in Lincolnshire and claim to have every style and size of antique bed under the sun at a range of prices – call 01507 603173 to arrange a time to visit (strictly by appointment only). Or for a real fairy-tale type you can have one hand-made by James Adam Furniture in Woodbridge, Suffolk. His Louis XVI-style four-poster frame in these dimensions would start from around £1,200. If that's a bit beyond the budget it might be worth trying a local carpenter to see if he can put one together more cheaply – I've seen DIY experts do some very clever things with broom handles and MDF: it's amazing what you can get away with once it's all covered in some draped fabric.

Q I am looking for a chair that will convert into a single bed for occasional visitors, as a sofa bed would be too big. Do you have any idea if such a thing exists?

A Yes it does (pity really, as it's such a good idea that it might have been the way to make your fortune), and several furniture shops seem to be cottoning on to it. Try Highly Sprung, who do seven different models of chair beds that have proper sprung mattresses – prices start at £699. Visit them at 185 Tottenham Court Road, London W1, or call 020 7924 1124 for your nearest

Jane Asher's

showroom or a brochure. Sofas & Sofa Beds (84–92 Tottenham Court Road, London W1, or call 020 7813 1490 for branches) make one for £459 plus 8 metres of fabric. If you need something even smaller, Sofa Workshop do something called a stool bed for £499 plus 4 metres of fabric. It's like a big camp bed that doubles as somewhere to rest your weary feet when your guests have gone. Telephone 01798 343400 for branches and a brochure.

Q My husband and I treated ourselves to a super king-sized bed recently. Because of its size, it's difficult enough to get bedding for it, but the real problem is how warm we both get during the night. I have already bought a new duvet and we have tried both cotton and polyester covers and sheets, yet we still wake up hot and bothered. Have you any suggestions?

A I can't quite see the connection between the size of your bed and the fact that you get too hot – unless you're having some very energetic fun in it now you've both got room to manoeuvre, in which case it seems a small price to pay. Or maybe the new mattress is covered in a man-made fabric – it might be worth buying a cotton cover to go over it. Otherwise, super king size bedding shouldn't be that tricky to find in large department stores as it's fairly standard nowadays, or try the Austrian Bedding Co who stock a wide range in your size. While I was chatting to them I mentioned your hot bed problem, and they have a possible solution – special duvets that can be opened up at the sides so that a layer of filling can be added or removed according to your needs. They're at 205 Belsize Road, London NW6, telephone 020 7372 3121.

Q I have a 4-foot bed and am having trouble finding sheets to fit it.

A I would suggest you try the London-based company Bedstock – 020 8964 1547.

Q My three-piece suite is in quite good condition, but the cushions need replacing. Can I do this, or do I have to re-upholster the whole thing?

A I would suggest you get in touch with a good upholsterer, who will be able to make cushions to fit. Start by contacting the Association of Master Upholsterers and Soft Furnishers, Frances Vaughan House, 102 Commercial Street, Newport, NP9 1LU, telephone 01633 215454. They will be able to recommend a company in your area.

Q With our summers in mind, I tried to order a patio heater from a garden catalogue recently, only to be told that they are unable to obtain them.

A You never know – it might be a glorious summer. But if you'd rather play safe, contact the American Trading Company on 020 8529 4616, which offers a range of patio heaters from about £399 plus VAT.

Q We recently visited a Bryant show house at Beacon Heights in Newark and were very impressed by a wallpaper in the dining room – a beige wainscot design with a matching border that had the appearance of a picture rail. Do you know who makes it and where we could buy it from?

A The decor was the work of interior designer Anne Sendall (0121 355 7263) and the paper is a pattern called Wolsey, by Osborne and Little. For your nearest stockist call 020 7352 1456.

Q I've just moved into a new house and really hate the existing kitchen units. The previous owners had the right idea about where everything should go, so the basic carcasses are in the right places, but our tastes are just poles apart. Can I leave the bare bones of the kitchen in place and replace just the doors?

A And it does matter, doesn't it? The kitchen is the heart of the house, and if you hate the surroundings it'll make you miserable. You'll be pleased to hear that your idea of changing just the doors is perfectly possible: James Mayor Furniture supplies a range of replacement doors in a number of styles from Shaker to metal mesh and from wired glass to gothic designs. All are made in MDF to any size and come either sanded or primed ready for painting. Prices depend on dimensions, style and finish. For a brochure, call JMF on 0121 643 8344. Then you can think about that bedroom wardrobe, and the bathroom cabinet . . .

Q **I have tried unsuccessfully to find out more about limestone flooring. Can you help?**

A You don't say where you want to put it, but bear in mind that limestone is heavy, so can only be laid on a base that is structurally sound – ideally, concrete or cement screed. If the existing floor is wood, it'll need to be strengthened beforehand. You also have to seal the stone properly – this is especially important if, for example, you want to put the limestone in your kitchen. The stone is naturally porous and so will need to be well protected from staining by grease and oil; in fact I was advised against it some years ago by a friend who had had trouble keeping it clean. We ignored her warnings and put it in our hall, and – apart from one disaster with black ink which meant replacing a tile – we've never looked back. I used UK Marble – ring them on 01432 352178. Limestone is also supplied by Fired Earth (01295 812088), Stone Age (020 7720 6556) or Stonell (01892 833500).

Q Why do manufacturers only make circular tablecloths with a small diameter? I have been trying for some time to find one with a diameter of 48 or 54 inches, and it has proved impossible.

A I came across this problem a few years ago and eventually gave up the search. We've lived with a table that has its skirt saucily showing far too much leg ever since. I have investigated further, and although I can't find out why there are so few around, I have managed to track down one source: round tablecloths up to 106 inches in diameter are available by post from The Linen Cupboard, 21 Great Castle Street, London W1. Their telephone number is 020 7629 4062. My table will be decent at last.

Q Please rescue me from the doghouse. While washing up, I dropped and broke my wife's mixing bowl. Extensive inquiries have failed to find a replacement. The bowl in question fits into a Braun KM32 mixer and has gear teeth on the inside of the upper rim.

A A number of companies stock Braun spares, and the ones I spoke to seem pretty confident that they'll be able to help you get back into your wife's good books. Call the Braun consumer helpline on 0800 783 7010. They'll need the model number, so keep the details handy when you contact them.

Q I have heard that there is a company that can find spare parts for electrical appliances. Do you know how I might contact them?

A The company I think you want is Spare by Post, which will track down spare parts for any type of gas or electrical appliance. Their telephone number is: 0117 939 8888. They will need the model number, so have the details handy when you contact them.

Q Over the years a few pieces of our wedding dinner service have been chipped or broken. I have an emotional attachment to the design and do not want to buy a different service, and although I have tried the big department stores no one seems to stock the line any longer.

A Oh, isn't it a shame when sets of crockery are no longer complete, especially when you have several guests to entertain or are missing that vital teapot lid? Don't despair – there are several china-matching companies you could try: Chinasearch, telephone 01926 512402; Tablewhere?, telephone 020 8671 4047, or the China Matching Service on 01548 531372.

Q I have moved into an old farmhouse and would like to have an 'authentic' looking sink, perhaps a butler's sink, for the utility room.

A Butler's ceramic sinks have become so trendy that many fitted kitchen companies include them in their ranges now, not to mention the usual hardware stores and builder's merchants, but if you fancy buying an old one with character then dealers in architectural salvage are the people to try. The best contact here is Salvo, who can give advice on where to find anything you might need for any aspect of house restoration anywhere in the country. An information pack that includes a listing of salvage dealers is available for £5.75 from Salvo, 18 Ford Village, Berwick upon Tweed, Northumberland TD15 2QG, telephone 01890 820333. You could also consider an enamelled cast iron sink: try Aston Matthews, 141/147A Essex Road, London N1, telephone 020 7226 3657.

Q **I have recently moved house and my new bathroom only includes a shower cubicle. On a recent holiday in Spain my apartment contained a small bath approximately 75 cm wide by 100 cm long, which would be ideal for my bathroom. Despite efforts throughout my local area I have been unable to track down anything similar over here.**

A I've found one that comes within a few centimetres – it's from Aston Matthews (020 7226 7220) and measures 73 cm wide by 108 cm long. It is available in white only and costs £149 plus VAT. Another option, made by Armitage Shanks, is called a Showertub – essentially, it's a small bath and shower-base all rolled into one and even includes a little seat. At around £222 plus VAT, it might be a good alternative as it would mean you could keep your shower unit as well as having the luxury of a proper soak from time to time. Call 01543 490253 for your nearest stockist.

Q Have you any idea where I can obtain some 'Victoriana Brown' wall tiles (6 inches square). I am aware that they might have been discontinued but wonder if you know of somewhere or someone who might have this particular design.

A I'm hoping you mean those plain brown tiles found around period fireplaces – if so, don't worry, because you can buy reproduction ones from Original Style for around £1 per tile – phone 01392 474054 for a catalogue and your nearest distributor. Otherwise, if you particularly want genuine ones, a local architectural salvage yard is a good place to try.

Q I have been looking everywhere for Reckitt's Blue Cubes. Where have they gone?

A Sadly these were discontinued years ago. Modern soap powders are supposed to be so good that you don't need them . . . well, that's the theory anyway.

Q I used to have a wonderful old-fashioned magnifying mirror attached to an arm over the bathroom basin, but it's recently been broken. Is it possible to find a new one?

A I have several companies you could try for a new magnifying mirror: Black Country Heritage, telephone: 01384 480810; Aero, telephone 020 7221 1950 or 020 8971 0066 for their mail order catalogue; Architectural Components, telephone 020 7581 2401.

Jane Asher's

Q Could you please help me find a shop that sells merino wool blankets – I can only find cellular ones.

A There's nothing quite like merino – it's particularly soft as well as being so warm. I'm delighted to see it reappearing in jumpers in High Street stores. Your luck's in, though, because these blankets are indeed still available from a company called Early's of Witney. Either call them on 01993 703131 to find out where your nearest stockist is, or visit their factory shop at Witney Mill, Witney, Oxon, OX8 5EB.

Q I am 15 years old and because of my baby brother's increasing need for space – namely needing his own room – I am to give up my bedroom and move in with my two younger sisters. Being a teenage girl, I would still like some privacy, so I am contemplating the idea of a screen to separate my bed from the rest of the room. Can you tell me where I can find a screen, preferably one which I could fold away when it isn't needed?

A You're being very accommodating about this – it does seem a bit unfair that there are three of you in one room and only one in the other, but I can see that it's a better option than sharing with the socks, football posters and testosterone. According to the style of the room you'll be moving into, you could choose a screen made in wicker or one with plain calico panels – both designs have a metal frame, three panels and fold up easily so they can be stored out of the way when necessary. The rattan screen costs

£99 from The Pier; telephone 020 7814 5004 for mail order. The calico is also £99 and comes from The Cotswold Company; telephone 01276 606029 for mail order.

FOOD

Q Where can I find the old Bournville Cocoa, the one with the brown and orange label? The others I have tried are tasteless and not the lovely dark brown original.

A The brown and orange packaging was changed to a purple tin with orange lettering some time ago, and its name was changed to Cadbury's Cocoa Powder. So if you've used that and you think it doesn't taste the same as the Bournville it must be your imagination (unless of course they've sneakily changed it without telling us). Try shutting your eyes as you open the tin.

Q Where can I buy macadamia nuts? I know you can get them in Australia, but that's a long way to go to satisfy my craving!

A I'm pleased to be able to save you a few hundred pounds and a dose of jet-lag. I've bought macadamia nuts in small packets from my local supermarket, but if you can't find them near you there's a snazzy company called Fifth Sense who supply all sorts of food by mail order including roasted and salted macadamia nuts. A 300-g/12-oz bag costs £5.60 plus p & p – to order, call 01846 628666.

Q Please can you help me find a supplier of smoked salmon, as I'd love to send some to a relative for Christmas. I would want the fish to be already sliced.

A It's such a great present – my mother sends us a side every year and we all love it. But don't leave it too late, as suppliers get very busy towards Christmas. She orders it from MacGilvray, Coldstreame Seafood, the Harbour, Whitstable, Kent CT5 1AB, telephone 01227 276722.

Q I am trying to organize some blue and white sugared almonds for my son's wedding. Locally, the wholesalers' colours are poor and if I buy decent quality ones retail they'll turn out very expensive. Do you know of a wholesaler who supplies them?

A You can get some great colours now – you always used to see them in just pink and white. The silver and gold are especially beautiful. Try Direct Confectionery, telephone 020 8444 1800, who ask for a minimum order of 1 kg. Alternatively, Davals, a sweet shop in Cheshire, can send out orders of any amount: telephone 01928 739911.

Q I like my tea very weak – just one dunk with a teabag. My mum says it's wasteful and wants me to re-use each one, but I think tea tastes horrible when it's made with a cold, soggy teabag. Can you back me up on this, and is there any kind of gadget that I can use that would keep my mum quiet?

Jane Asher's

A Yes I certainly can back you up on the re-using issue. There is something especially unattractive about used teabags, and even if it doesn't affect the taste I don't think you should be expected to use them more than once. After all you're not really being wasteful – however weak or strong you like your tea, the ratio of one bag to one cup is the same. There are a couple of other alternatives for making single cups, though: there is a natty little gadget like a perforated spoon, double sided and hinged, into which you put a small amount of loose tea. It goes in a cup in the same way as a bag would, and you simply stir, and then lift it out when the tea is strong enough. They came out during the First World War before tea bags were invented, and they are still available at Whittard of Chelsea, who supply them by mail order for £2.50 each. Ring 020 7924 1888 and ask for a 'long-handled infuser'. Or you could always resort to instant tea granules – but I think they taste so disgusting it's hardly worth it.

Q **I recently won a popcorn-making machine and in the instructions it tells me that I should use popcorn maize to get the best results. It also states that I should use a standard grade, as premium or gourmet grades have too vigorous a popping action. I have tried to obtain these goods from supermarkets and health shops in my area but have had no joy.**

A Bags of maize kernels should be available pretty widely – I've checked with both Tesco and Sainsbury and they certainly do stock them. But if you can't find it locally then Jerry's Home

Tricks of the Trade

Store, who specialize in American products, sell what they claim is the best popping corn ever. It is called White Cat Corn and costs £3.95 a jar; to order it by post, call 020 7581 0909.

Q **I never seem to find good marmalade. It is either too runny or comes out of the jar like a blob of jelly. Can you recommend one with a good consistency and flavour?**

A It's a very personal business, marmalade. I'm a bit of a wimp and like mine golden and soft with small bits in it; my husband likes his tawny and strong, with huge chunks of rind. My favourite is homemade by my sister's mother-in-law – but that's a fat lot of use to anyone outside my family. You may find a local WI branch that sells home-made marmalade, but as a second choice I'd go for Frank Cooper's Oxford marmalade for the dark sort and Wilkins Tiptree Medium Cut for a less butch type.

Q **I recently saw a television programme featuring HRT cakes. Where can I get them?**

A I know the cake you mean – apparently, a slice a day was meant to cure all the unpleasant side-effects of the menopause. It sounds too good to be true, and in a way it is, according to nutrition expert Maryon Stewart at the Women's Nutritional Advisory Service. The cake contains what are known as phytoestrogens (a family of naturally occurring substances similar to the female hormone oestrogen) which are found in foods such as linseeds,

Jane Asher's

soya and pulses. Phytoestrogens can help regulate hormone levels, giving a boost and protecting us against, among other things, the dreaded hot flushes – Nature's charming way of telling us we're not needed for child-bearing any more, thanks very much. Stewart says that eating just one slice of this special cake a day isn't going to be enough – but combine it with other dietary changes, certain nutritional supplements and an exercise and relaxation regime, and it may help with post-menopausal symptoms. More details and many phyto-rich recipes can be found in *The Phyto Factor* by Maryon Stewart (Vermilion, £8.99). For an information pack and a leaflet about phytoestrogens, send six loose first-class stamps and an A5 SAE, marking the envelope 'midlife onwards', to The Women's Nutritional Advisory Service, PO Box 268, Lewes, East Sussex BN7 2QN.

ANTIQUES

Q My grandmother recently left me a little 5-inch geisha figurine (slightly chipped) in what I think is ivory. Where is the best place to check whether it is, and to advise me on how to get it mended?

A You need someone called a conservator. The best way to find the right one is through the Museums & Galleries Commission, whose Conservation Register lists more than 600 conservators throughout the UK, one of whom is bound to be able to verify the date of the statue and then restore it as necessary. By telephoning 020 7233 4220, and for a fee of £5, details of five conservators specializing in the required field will be supplied (local to you whenever possible) – a useful service to remember whenever you need to find the right person to help bring the most obscure antiques back to life. If your heirloom turns out to be a plastic geisha that your granny won at the fair last year, you'll just have to put it down to experience.

Q My mother has a beautiful tortoiseshell box she was given long ago as an engagement gift. She uses it to keep knick-knacks in, but over the years it has become chipped and worn. She has expressed regret about this, so as a birthday present for her I would like to have it made as good as new. Where can I find someone to help?

Jane Asher's

A There is a company based in London that specializes in antique boxes, and tortoiseshell in particular, so they will be able to advise you on restoration. They are called Halcyon Days and are based at 14 Brook Street, London W1. Their telephone number is 020 7629 0280.

Q **I have inherited two old gunpowder flasks. Unfortunately the tops are missing and I am keen to find replacements.**

A I suggest you get in touch with Blunderbuss Antiques, who are arms specialists. Their address is 29 Thayer Street, London W1, telephone 020 7486 2444. If they can't help you, try Manfred Schotten, the sporting antiques dealers – 109 High Street, Burford, Oxfordshire, telephone 01993 822302.

CLOTHES

Q Any idea where I can buy a pair of size 5 chest-high fishing-type boots (preferably by mail order)? My garden pond is due for a tidy up and my wellies aren't long enough to prevent me getting wet feet.

A This isn't going to be cheap: chest-high fishing-type boots (or waders as they are far more boringly called by the pros) are available from angling shops such as Farlow's at 5 Pall Mall, London SW1, telephone 020 7839 2423. They cost around £69.95 and can be posted if you can't make it up to town. There are many different types, so call for advice – presumably there's a special anti-green slime and pond weed variety that would suit.

Q Any ideas where I can buy real silk stockings, ideally by mail order?

A Oooh! Most of us have got used to making do with a polyamid/elastane mix, but I admit it doesn't sound as sexy as silk. No one in the UK manufactures them, so that's why you've had problems. However, a company called Agent Provocateur stocks them in black for £20 and can supply by mail order (020 7253 5123). But for goodness' sake don't ladder them as you put them on – at £10 a leg it could get expensive.

Jane Asher's

Q My grandson is 6 foot 6 inches tall with a slim waist. He has just landed a summer job as a waiter, but is having trouble finding trousers long enough in the leg that don't drown him.

A It might be worth trying the gentlemen's outfitters, High and Mighty, who do white shirts and black trousers in fairly small waist measurements. These may well do for your grandson. Ring 01488 684666 for nationwide branches.

Q Where can I buy a Kangol waterproof hat?

A Call Kangol Hats Ltd on 020 7487 4888 and the company will be happy to give you details of your nearest stockist.

Q I am a 17-year-old student with a slim figure – and a 34E bust. My problem is that all the bras I can find in large cup sizes are, frankly, matronly. What I want is something low-cut, sexy and pretty – and hopefully not too ruinously expensive. I've tried a mail order firm, but with disappointing results. Am I asking the impossible? Or does no one understand that we well-endowed girls don't want to look like Amazons in our underwear?

A Rigby & Peller, the very smartest of lingerie retailers, say that there's no reason why you shouldn't find exactly what you're looking for, but they feel that it's important to be properly measured so that you get a bra that fits perfectly. (I went there once to be fitted for a corset for a period drama – it is the most wonderful shop, and for a special treat you might think about investing in one of their beautiful bras.) But for everyday wear Gossard make several designs which should be perfect. What about the enticing-sounding 'Gypsy' in lipstick pink? It's lacy, low-cut, available in your size and costs around £22 from all the usual department stores. Or the broderie anglaise-decorated 'Carmen', or the stretch lace 'Etoile' . . . My advice is to look in the High Street and you'll find what you're looking for.

Q I cannot find any Double-A fitting shoes and am getting quite desperate. I've heard of a factory near Leeds that sells them to the public, but I don't know the name.

A What a slim and elegant foot you must have – surely a glass slipper gently fitted by a prince is what you deserve? If a prince isn't around, try the Directory of Footwear for Special Needs. Send a cheque for £3, payable to BFA, with your name and address on the back, to the British Footwear Association, 5 Portland Place, London W1N 3AA. (What an extraordinarily apt postcode!)

Q I walk in such a way so as to make my shoes gape at the instep. What can I do about this?

A Try buying some small arch cushions which are made by Dasco. If you telephone them on 01536 760760 they will be able to give you the details of your nearest stockist.

Q My feet are odd sizes: one is size 9 and the other size 10, so I usually wear pairs that are either too large or too small for one of my feet. It would be too expensive to have shoes hand-made for me, so please don't suggest that. And the prospect of scrabbling through piles of shoes in the Sales doesn't appeal. Is there a shop for people like me?

A Yes, there is indeed a shop you could try. It has the rather comforting name of Sole Mates, and can be found at 46 Gordon Road, Chingford, London, E4 6BU. If you send them an SAE they will help you find shoes in different sizes.

Q My father has been complaining of blisters on his feet where the seams of his socks chafe against his skin. Is there such a thing as seamless socks?

A Yes there is. I would suggest you try outdoor pursuits shops – they sell tube-knitted seamless ones (seams cause blisters for walkers, skiers and climbers too!).

Q The ever-popular component of Lycra in socks causes my feet to overheat and produces a condition similar to either severe athlete's foot or chilblains. My elderly, pure cotton socks are giving up the struggle but I can't seem to find anywhere to buy this endangered species.

A Anyone who lives in a house with three enormous males as I do has a life partly dominated by giant socks. You can certainly get all-cotton men's socks in many department stores, but for ladies' ones I can recommend those from Natural Fact (they even make them in organically grown cotton and hemp: the socks are free-range and reared in open pens with access to – no, sorry, I'm getting carried away here). They come in a range of colours including ecru, black, light brown and navy, and prices start at £4.99. Cotton tights are also available, just in case you really feel the cold. The shop is at 192 King's Road, London SW3. A mail order service is available – call on 020 7352 2227 for more details.

Q I recently returned from a trip to Canada with a new pair of Levi's for my boyfriend. When he tried them on I realized that I had got the wrong size. When I tried to exchange them here I found that no one would exchange them because they were bought abroad. I don't understand this, but is there anything I can do or, unless my boyfriend loses a few stone, am I out of pocket for good?

A How extremely irritating. The problem is that, although they're an international brand, many of the shops you'll have visited will have been franchises, which can't deal with the different labels and bar-codes your jeans will be carrying. The solution is to go to the main Levi's flagship store in London's Regent Street (you can post them if necessary) where they should be able to exchange them for you. That's certainly an easier option than making your boyfriend eat lettuce for a month.

Jane Asher's

Q I am trying to find some storage bags that are made of cotton or linen (not plastic) that I can fill with clothes and put on top of the wardrobe to save some space inside my cupboards.

A Although you never quite know about the English summer it's a great feeling to get bulky sweaters and thick jackets out of the way as long as you hang on to the odd cardy or two (back in fashion, I hear). The Holding Company supplies some attractive cream-coloured canvas bags with wire frames that are just the right size to fill with jumpers and so on and will easily slip on top of a wardrobe or even under the bed. They cost £14.95 each. Call 020 7610 9160 to order by post.

GIFTS

Q My father is 90 this year and we are having a big celebration, so my family and I have been trying to come up with a gift idea that is unusual yet special. My son, who is a keen gardener (as my father used to be) suggested that we get a rose named after him. Have you any idea how we might go about this?

A There are two ways, the first of which is likely to be rather expensive (we're talking thousands) as it involves approaching a professional rose breeder and putting the rose on the commercial market. A cheaper alternative is to approach an amateur breeder who is raising new seedlings. For about £500 you should get 10 of 'your' roses plus a certificate. The timing of your gift will obviously depend on what he or she is growing and whether there is time to do the necessary grafting to produce the 10 plants by the date in question. It would make a wonderful present, though. For more details and a list of breeders, contact Derrick Everitt, Secretary of the Amateur Rose Breeder's Association, 48 Shrewsbury Fields, Shifnal, Shropshire TF11 8AN. He'll deserve a very special cake, too, of course. To order a personalized one by mail ring my shop on 020 7584 6177.

Q Could you please help me to find a present for my friend's pearl wedding anniversary? I was thinking of perhaps getting something in mother-of-pearl for use at their table.

Jane Asher's

A

There's a mail order catalogue called House that offers mother-of-pearl accessories which are just the thing. There's a set of six decorative spoons (£17.95), a small dish with a tiny fork and spoon (£18.95), and a salt and pepper set (£9.95). All prices exclude p & p. For a catalogue or to order, telephone 01725 552549.

Q

I have been asked to be godmother to my baby niece and would rather not take a silver bracelet or an engraved tankard. Can you suggest a chic, meaningful gift?

A

Some shops which appear very expensive have unusual little presents that cost far less than you might think. For instance, Tiffany's mail order service (Tiffany Touch: 020 7499 4577) has everything from china piggy banks in pink or blue polka dots at £45 to a silver birth record frame which can have baby's name, date and weight engraved on it for £220. There's nothing quite like one of those exquisite pale turquoise boxes tied with white ribbon, and although the baby won't appreciate it, it'll mean a lot to her parents. Or try Harvey Nichols: they suggest an unusual and cute Christofle silver-plated hinged egg designed to keep the child's first tooth as a keepsake (£55). I was so impressed when my brother laid down some port to celebrate the birth of one of our boys that when a friend of mine had a girl I talked to Berry Bros and Rudd, who suggested some sweet dessert wine, ready to drink when she's 18 or 21. Any good wine merchant will recommend a case or half-case to suit your budget.

BITS AND BOBS

Q My fiancé and I are planning to get married while white-water rafting down the Zambezi river in Zimbabwe – the trip is for a charity supporting children with cerebral palsy (SCOPE). We are expected to raise £2,500 each and are looking for ways to raise the money. We don't believe that we should be asking everyone for £1 here and 50p there – mainly because people don't seem to be as interested in charity as much as they used to be. We need an approach that stands out – maybe approaching outfits with relevant interests, such as wet suit manufacturers or companies with a young, sporty outlook. Any ideas?

A The vicars out there must have very good balance, mustn't they? But you are brave: I hear the white-water rafting on the Zambezi is terrifying. I'm not sure I agree that people are less interested in charity nowadays – I never fail to be moved by the British public's generosity – but there's certainly so much competition that you do indeed need a way of making your appeal stand out. Your idea of approaching companies with some sort of connection is good. Remember they'll need to get something out of it in return: even if as individuals they are philanthropic, as businesses their generosity needs to be cost effective. Offer to stick their logo on the raft or ask a local celebrity to put on one of their wet suits and present the cheque to you: something that can get a picture in the local paper or a mention on the radio – you know the sort

Jane Asher's

of thing. Meanwhile, I wouldn't totally discount the small donations; they can add up surprisingly quickly. The good old sponsorship form still works wonders.

My daughter would like to collect stamps for the Cat's Protection League. How do I go about converting the stamps into funds?

Don't worry about converting them first – if you send the stamps direct to the charity, they can do the rest. They save up all the donations from kind people such as your daughter until they have enough, then sell them on by the kilo to their own contacts. So she can start collecting (remembering to leave a small border around each stamp) and then post them to the CPL at 17 Kings Road, Horsham, West Sussex, RH13 5PN.

Why is it that I cannot find the red AIDS ribbons anywhere at the moment? Can you tell me which shops stock them?

The ribbons are sold all over the place during the run-up to World Aids Day on December 1, but at other times can be hard to find, although branches of HIV and AIDS groups stock them all year round. Your nearest group can be contacted on 01473 232007 (lines staffed during working hours). Otherwise, for anyone wanting a supply of ribbons for fund-raising purposes, simply contact the makers, Red Ribbon International, who are at City Cloisters, 188–194 Old Street, London EC1V 9FR. I've sometimes made my own at the last minute when I wanted to show support, but it's important not to forget to donate money to accompany the gesture if you do.

Q I was recently given a set of Russian dolls bought as a gift from Kiev. My four granddaughters love playing with them and fitting each doll inside each other. I'd like to collect different shapes and sizes, but where can I buy them in this country?

A You'll find a selection of different styles and designs at The Russia House, 55 Southwark Street, London SE1, telephone 020 7450 3262 (prices from £3 for a three-piece doll). Alternatively, sets of up to 10 nesting dolls (which are pricier but presumably more covetable to collectors like yourself) are on sale at The Russian Shop, The Arches, Villiers Street, London WC2, telephone 020 7930 3484. I bet it's not just the granddaughters who enjoy playing with them – it's the little tiny one in the very middle that's my favourite.

Q I have been trying to trace a stockist of a perfume called Je Reviens, by Worth, but without success. I read somewhere that it was a favourite scent of yours and wonder if you could tell me where I might buy it?

A It's more than just a favourite – I wear it every day. I dabble with others but always come back to it – without it I just wouldn't smell like me any more. Yes, it can be hard to find: I've been wearing it since I was 17 and when I ask for it at some beauty

212

counters the assistants raise their perfectly groomed eyebrows as if I were asking for woad. Harrods still stock it and there's often a special offer of a triple pack in duty free. Or order it by post from Beauty Base, 151 Queensway, London, W2, telephone 020 7229 5600. Anyone else trying to track down an elusive perfume could try the Cosmetic, Toiletry and Perfume Association on 020 7491 8891. They have information on whether various perfumes are still manufactured.

Q A friend of mine who lives abroad was interviewed for a documentary produced by the BBC. I promised to record it for him, but I was on holiday when it was transmitted. How can I get hold of a copy?

A The BBC have a helpline to track down information about programmes transmitted on the network. If you telephone them on 08700 100222 they will be able to assist you.

Q I do the make-up for our local amateur dramatics group. The only powder puffs I seem to be able to find in chemists are too small – do larger ones exist?

A There is a company called Screenface based in London who sell larger powder puffs. Their address is 48 Monmouth Street, London WC2, telephone 020 7836 3955. In fact you may well be able to find other essential backstage supplies you didn't know you needed!

Q We still do (occasionally!) have hot summer days, but why does no one sell parasols? I for one would find such an item most useful, and have searched everywhere – to no avail.

A I quite agree – and one feels rather silly carrying an umbrella about on a sunny day. It seems they are not generally sold these days due to lack of demand, but it is worth you contacting a theatre and film costume house as they provide them for period pieces. Try Angels & Bermans, 40 Camden Street, London NW1, telephone 020 7387 0999.

Q I was reading an interesting article in an old copy of Life magazine in my dentist's recently. I would like to try to get hold of it, but perhaps the magazine no longer exists?

A Yes, *Life* magazine does still exist. You need to contact the back issues department at: Life Magazine, Time Inc, Time-Life Building, Rockefeller Centre, 1271 Avenue of the Americas, New York 10020, USA. Telephone 001 212 522 1212.

Q Is there any way I can have re-pleated a favourite old skirt that has lost its crispness after years of wear?

A There are a couple of companies who do permanent pleating: F Ciment Pleating Ltd, telephone 020 8520 0415, and Instyle Pleaters, telephone 020 8986 6991. Give them a call and they will advise you how to proceed.

Q My 15-year-old granddaughter has the most beautiful long, slim hands and nails which she takes great care of. I think she might stand a chance of being a hand model. Is there an agency that specializes in this sort of work?

A I wish I could use a hand model in real life – mine are always in a terrible state. It's certainly worth your granddaughter having a go. There are a couple of hand model agencies in London, but a more general agency often deals with this sort of work, too. To find one in your area look in your local Yellow Pages. The company concerned will probably ask you to send in some photographs, then it's a case of fingers (beautifully) crossed.

Q As an avid fan of talking books, due to failing sight, I would be interested to know of any rental, second-hand or trading services for these tapes. My library's choice is very limited.

A I'm a fan of them too: in my case, on long car journeys. The Royal National Institute for the Blind offers a talking book service for those with sight problems. It costs £54 for a year but you can choose an unlimited number of books during that time. A staggering three million are issued each year. Call 020 8903 6666 for details.

Q My daughter, who is 20, is left-handed and has never been able to use an ordinary pair of scissors. She has had one special pair since she was five years old, but they've seen better days. Any idea where I could replace them?

A I've tracked down a brilliant catalogue called Anything Left Handed which, appropriately enough, opens backwards (or forwards as far as your daughter is concerned, of course) and includes among other things a range of specially designed scissors for tasks ranging from dressmaking and paper cutting to trimming nails and hair. Apparently, it's well worth getting the correct tools for the job, because right-handed scissors mean that she would have to look over the top of the blade to see where she's cutting – an awkward manoeuvre. Once she gets into it, there's no end of gadgetry she'll discover she can't live without – left-handed potato peelers, corkscrews, tin openers, ladles . . . even a boomerang. To order by credit card, call 020 8770 3722, or visit the shop at 57 Brewer Street, London W1.

Q We recently visited the Champagne region of France and brought back several bottles in anticipation of the millennium and other family celebrations that year. We do not have a cellar, so how should we best store the champagne? We saw some special wine coolers for sale in French supermarkets, but they were the size of an upright fridge-freezer and so were too big to transport back by car. Can you buy them over here? We were advised that an ordinary fridge would be too cold. Otherwise, what do you suggest, apart from digging a big hole in our garden and using that?

Jane Asher's

A You can, indeed, buy the wine coolers over here – a company called EuroCave (020 8200 1266) produces a range that will store between 38 and 240 bottles of wine or champagne in just the right conditions. But they're very expensive (starting at around £750). According to the Champagne Information Bureau, there are several golden rules to follow when keeping bubbly. The most surprising advice is that you don't have to lie it down: whereas still wines need to be on their sides to keep the corks moist, the bubbles in champagne do the job for you even when it's vertical. It's crucial to keep it out of daylight and at a constant, cool temperature, so, if you decide to give that special cooler a miss, I'm told that a sealed box kept somewhere that's well away from kitchens and boilers is as good as anything. An unheated, windowless garage is often a good place – a solution that will also save you a lot of digging. Non-vintage, by the way, should keep well for six months to a year, so that should be OK for the Millennium. If you bought all non-vintage then you'll just have to drink it all up and buy more for the celebrations later in the year. Poor you, what a terrible thought.

Q **I have a large doll that was brought back from Italy 35 years ago for my daughter. Unfortunately, her leg was sat on and got broken. A friend tried to repair it without success, so the poor doll has been in a box for a long time. Do you know anyone who could bring her back to life?**

Tricks of the Trade

You need to find the address of your nearest dolls' hospital – for a list of repairers in your area, send for The UK Doll Directory, which is available for £5.60 (inc p & p) from PO Box 290, Brighton, BN2 1DR, or by calling Huggets Publishing on 01273 697974 and asking for the Doll Directory. I advise you to keep well out of that doll's way once she's better: how would you like to be shut in a cardboard box for several years with a broken leg?

Q

My husband and I are visiting America in September to stay with my pen-friend and her family. I know that she would like me to take over a Paddington Bear, but despite many enquiries I have not been able to buy one.

A

You'll find him resting in Hamleys – lots of him, in fact. They have little ones, big ones, ones in boots, ones with bags and ones wearing duffle coats . . . so there should be no problem getting what you're looking for. For mail order, ring 020 7494 2000 and ask for customer services.

Q

Would you know whom I should contact so that I do not constantly receive piles of unwanted mail? I feel it is such a waste of paper, plus people's time delivering it – and subsequently the refuse men taking it to the tip.

A

You're so right – it's absurd how much of our family's morning post goes straight in the bin. Mind you, there's still a pathetic little bit of me that gets very excited when I read: 'MRS SCARFE –

YOU ARE ON OUR SPECIAL SHORTLIST OF ONLY 5 MILLION PEOPLE TO RECEIVE OUR STAR PRIZE' and suchlike. But yes – it can be stopped, via the Mailing Preference Service, who can short-circuit anything that is addressed to you personally, which means up to 95% of the piles of junk that usually get stuffed through your letterbox. You should allow at least three months for the volume of junk mail to decrease, and after that your name will remain on file for 5 years and you should have cracked the problem. The only things that will still get through are those addressed 'To the occupier', plus hand-delivered items. To register and save all those trees, call 0345 034599 or write with your full name, address and postcode to MPS, Freepost 22, London W1E 7EZ. Alternatively, you could always recycle your junk mail for charity.

Q **I gave my e-mail address to a rather lonely ex-girlfriend of a friend of mine. I am now on her 'joke' list, and receive dubious shaggy dog jokes at work several times a day. Can I screen them out, or is there a way I could tactfully ask her to stop sending them to me?**

A I'm still new enough to e-mail to be thrilled when I switch on my computer and find a little unopened envelope ready for me, even when it turns out to be my service provider telling me what wonderful new facilities it has on offer. I can only suggest in your case that you tell her that the jokes are making you laugh so much that it's distracting you from your work and that, much as you hate to do it, you're going to have to ask her to send them out of office hours. A few seconds spent deleting them when you arrive in the morning should save any embarrassment for you and avoid hurting her feelings. I have also heard that most e-mail systems for Acorns, Apples and PCs allow you to filter mail from certain addresses or domains. Ask your network administrator or IT department.

Q **My children have grown up and I would like to start my own business. My idea is to buy designer clothes from various outlets as cheaply as possible (ends of lines, seconds, etc.) and then sell them myself here in the north. My husband hopes to retire in two years, so he could come with me all over the country to sales. I know I could make a success of it, providing I could find the right outlets, so wondered if you could help me locate them.**

A I must warn you to be very, very careful: when I started my own cake business nine years ago I had no idea what I was in for, and I spent countless wakeful nights worrying whether we'd ever be able to pay off the loan and make a go of it. However carefully you do the business plans and cash flow projections, reality always takes you by surprise, so do make sure you get good reliable advice before you commit yourself to any expenditure. But the idea is excellent and you're obviously very confident and enthusiastic, which is half the battle. You might well qualify for help from the Business Start-up Scheme which supports new enterprises launched by people who were not previously in paid work – more details from your local Citizens' Advice Bureau or town hall. As far as the clothing outlets go, two books should get you started: *The Bargain Hunter's Bible* (published by The Good Deal Directory, £9.99) and *The Factory Shopping and Sightseeing Guide to the UK* (same publisher, £3.99). Both will point you in the right direction to discount warehouses and so on.

Q **My husband and I both have arthritis and find it difficult to bleed our radiators with the small brass key we have. We have tried to find something with more grip, so far unsuccessfully.**

A I find those keys hard to use too – especially as the little buttons on the ends of radiators always seem to fuse themselves successfully with the rest of the metal. There's a mail order company called Keep Able which specializes in gadgets for people with problems such as this – their miraculous-sounding Contour Multi-Purpose Turner should do the trick, providing there's space beside the radiator to manoeuvre – you turn it with both hands, which takes the pressure off your fingers. It costs £10.39 plus VAT (from which you may be exempt) and p & p. Telephone 0990 202122 to order one or get a copy of their free catalogue. And, as a Vice President of Arthritis Care, I can recommend ringing the charity on 020 7916 1500 for more information on topics such as this.

Q **My daughter's school wants to put two pieces of her GCSE art-work on permanent display. Before they do this she would like to get good-quality colour copies of them. Locally we cannot find anyone who makes copies larger than A3 and these**

pictures are A2. Can you suggest anywhere in London or the southeast of England?

A

I thought this would be easy until I made a few calls on your behalf – it really is a specialist job. Eventually I came across a company that can do this sort of colour copying: St Albans Photoprint, Photoprint House, Stonecross, St Albans, AL1 4AA, telephone 01727 850777. Call to make an appointment first and expect to pay around £22 plus VAT per copy.

Q

I am trying to find a set of bagpipes to use at a party I am giving for my husband. He loves Scottish music and I'm sure would like to hang on to them afterwards. I have tried several music shops and have even written to the Scottish Tourist Board, but the cheapest ones I could find were £200.

A

I've managed to find some for £135, which is a bit of an improvement on your existing quote, from folk instrument specialists Hobgoblin Music (01293 515858), who have branches nationwide, including in your area. They're obviously fairly complex bits of equipment, so unless you come across a friend who has a set gathering dust in their attic, that's probably about the best price you'll find. If this is still too much, how about hiring a piper for the evening? Look under 'Weddings' in your local Yellow Pages. You obviously wouldn't be left with a set of pipes at the end of it, but that might not be altogether a bad thing: although I enjoy the sound of the pipes at the right moment, a little does go rather a long way, if you know what I mean...

Jane Asher's

Q My nephew is getting married in a few months' time and his mother and I would like to make our own special invitations using parchment paper. After extensive enquiries we can only obtain invitations that are already made up, and this is costly. Where can we can buy the raw materials?

A Real parchment is made from the skin of a sheep, goat or other animal, so I'm not surprised that it's expensive and rather thin on the ground. What you need is imitation parchment, and you can get it at London Graphic Centre (mail order available: call 020 7240 0095). It is available in various shades (including cream, green and blue) and costs 59p for a sheet measuring just under A1 size. I think cream sounds the most realistic – you don't see many green sheep around these days, do you?

Q How do I go about getting my novel published?

A I'm afraid it just entails sending off copies to as many publishers as possible (it took me eight with my first cake book!).

Q Where can I obtain a device that puts those plastic tag things through clothes? I am toying with the idea of selling second-hand clothes (all mine!) at a flea market or car boot sale, but want to label everything properly.

A They're called tagging guns and come in a variety of shapes and sizes. Unless you're labelling very delicate fabrics such as silk and satin, which can only cope with having especially small holes made in them, or very thick fabrics that need something altogether meatier, a standard gauge gun should be fine. The prices are pretty reasonable: the guns themselves start from around £9.99, then you'll have to pay around £5 for 5,000 tag attachments (I assume that'll be just about enough to cover your fashion mistakes?) All are available from Morplan, telephone 0800 451122. Unless you're particularly keen on labelling your fingers, it might be a good idea to spend £11.99 on a special protective tagging glove while you're at it.

Q I am secretly in love with a male friend of mine (and I think it might be mutual) and so am looking forward to the fact that I can finally show him some sign of affection on Valentine's Day. I'd like to send him something more than just a card – do you think that it's OK these days to send a man flowers?

A I expect it's very new-man-ish to send flowers but it somehow jars with me – even if it's something very butch like a cactus. How about a bottle of something, or a balloon? Or both? Just Balloons (020 7434 3039) can post out balloons to anywhere in the country. When your beloved opens the candy-striped box a helium heart-shaped balloon will float out, carrying your special message (cost: £14.69). The firm also does a bottle of Moet and a balloon by post for £59.93. For just a bottle, call Drinks Direct on 0800 232221. The firm can deliver anything from its brochure for the basic cost of the product plus £5.99.

Q **I have always wanted to improve my speech and can now afford lessons. Whom should I go to?**

A Call the Society of Teachers of Speech and Drama (01623 627636) which will put you in touch with members in your area, or look under speech and language therapists in the Yellow Pages.

HEALTH & BEAUTY

Nowadays we are bombarded by advice in the media about every aspect of health, beauty and general well-being, and with all the contradictory messages about what we should eat, drink, smother on our faces or take as supplements it can be hard to know just what to believe. I'm the first to be seduced by claims of wonder drugs or miracle beauty aids, but I do try to remind myself that as soon as a new scientific breakthrough has been thoroughly tested, evaluated and proven we shall surely be made aware of it. You can see all the cosmetic manufacturers quickly producing variations on a theme once there is evidence for a new approach to skin creams, for example – whether it's the properties of fruit acids or the power of anti-oxidants. And your GP should be the first to tell you of the usefulness of new diets or drugs once their effective-ness has been satisfactorily demonstrated.

But that's not to say there is no place for keeping up with the latest news on the beauty pages or in the medical columns: I read them with interest and, while trying to provide my family with the kind of diet that seems on balance to give them the best chance of health, enjoy keeping myself reasonably up to date on current thinking. I do, however, take some of the more exotic and dramatic revelations with a pinch of salt (remembering to make it a small pinch for the sake of low blood pres-sure, of course), as we've all seen the U-turns in theories about the ben-efits of sunshine, coffee, red wine and so on. As a doctor's daughter I was brought up to be pretty cynical about 'dramatic breakthroughs', and wary of the promise of mystical or unproven 'cures' – particularly if they necessitate the spending of hard-earned cash.

Q Do you have a cure for garlic breath? It would save my relationship if you did, as my girlfriend can't bear it.

A No, I wish I did. I don't believe any of the chewing parsley-type ideas really work. I don't think it necessarily means having to give up garlic for life – try using a little less and cooking it a little more and things may improve. It's the raw stuff that's the real killer. Otherwise it's garlic or her, I'm afraid.

Q I absolutely love black pepper, but on more than one occasion I have heard that too much is bad for you. Do you think this is true? If so, why?

A Is there anything edible left at all that isn't rumoured to doom us to one dreadful death or another? The pepper one is news to me, and I'm pleased to say that the toxicologists at the Ministry of Agriculture, Fisheries and Food say that it won't do you any harm at all – unless you use weirdly large amounts, which applies to almost everything. I always use delicious black pepper in and on everything and never the tasteless white dusty alternative.

Q We're continually being told to eat five portions of fruit and vegetables a day. I'm sure that one apple, one banana or one pear count as one portion each, but what about strawberries, raspberries or grapes?

Jane Asher's

A The Health Education Authority's advice is to eat five portions of fruit *or* veg each day. The quantities are as follows: apples, bananas, pears – one; grapefruit – $^1/_2$; plums – two; grapes and berries – one teacupful; salad, one dessert bowlful, peas and carrots (fresh or frozen) – 2 tbsp, broccoli and cauliflower – 2 oz (50 g); fruit juices – one glass.

Q **My son is 11, and one day he is bound to want to know how to shave properly. Silly as it sounds, I don't know. I'd dearly love to know the rules because I do not have a dad to ask . . . but my son does.**

A I'm sure it's very non-politically correct to talk in terms of 'girly' and 'boyish' information to get you through life, but until we're all cloned asexually and the differences disappear, this seems an extremely sensible and considerate question. I asked Ian Matthews, a barber who set up the world's first school of shaving in London (so you see you're not the only one) who says you score 10 out of 10 just for asking, as many men don't make the most of good grooming to look and feel their best. Ian recommends that first you soften the bristles by taking a shower before you shave and massaging the beard with water. Second, lift and lubricate the bristle with a brush and a rich shaving cream or gel. Third, use either a Gillette Mach 3 or Sensor razor – much experimenting has convinced him that these give the best results: if you've softened the bristles properly, you'll get 7–10 shaves out of each blade. Fourth, always glide the razor in the direction of growth, never against it; this gives a close shave, but if it's still not close enough, re-lather and shave across the grain, stopping if you feel any irritation. Fifth, rinse the skin with cool water and pat dry – never rub. Lastly, apply alcohol-free after-shave balm to replace the skin's natural oils. One-to-one consultations with Ian cost £35 per hour and will fill in any other fatherly pieces of advice your son may need about manly grooming. Call 020 7499 4904 for an appointment.

Q **My 16-year-old son is going on a sea-fishing holiday. He is very excited about it, but he suffers badly from motion sickness. Can you suggest any sure-fire remedies he could try?**

A Poor guy – the only other feeling that comes anywhere near the misery of seasickness is morning sickness, but at least he won't have to suffer that. This is one of those conditions where strange remedies pop out of the woodwork: I've been told he should try slipping copper pennies in the soles of his shoes, snacking on crystallized ginger and sitting on a pile of newspaper. The only quirky one that I have family experience of is wearing acupressure bands on both wrists. They really did appear to help my niece, and they are available from chemists. Otherwise, my own tip is that he keeps out on deck as much as possible – going below makes it much worse. (My theory is that if your brain can consciously see why your body is lurching about it can make sense of it and doesn't try to compensate and make you feel sick.) The other obvious option is to get some anti-motion sickness tablets from the chemist.

Q Like you I am a fellow redhead. I should like to know what moisturizing face and body lotions you recommend. There are many creams and lotions on the market and I have tried numerous, but many irritate rather than assist my skin.

A Although my skin is freckly and ridiculously pale (at school it was always easy to fake illness in Geography lessons) it doesn't react too badly to average creams, so I've never had to stick to the supposedly non-allergenic ranges. There's no question, though, that my face seems to prefer certain types to others, and over the years I've tended to use the Clinique 3-step system – wash, tone, moisturize – topped up with whichever latest wonder cream has advertised cleverly enough to fool me into believing its claims. The body lotion that seems to work best on my dry skin is Vaseline Intensive Care.

Q My 16-year-old daughter has started using my Estée Lauder moisturizer with extravagant abandon. How can I persuade her to use a cheaper one?

A We all suspect that own-brand cosmetics are just as good as the more expensive ones (many are made by the same factories) and yet we go on spending on the fancy packaging and classy names. I'm a sucker for all the beauty house claims. But if you believe them, do you want your daughter to use something less good? If you really feel she'd be just as well off with a cheaper one, I suspect you secretly know that you would, too. Perhaps you could get her to use less: Estée Lauder herself apparently recommended using tiny amounts of her creams. She advised clients to put the date of purchase on the base and note how long it lasted, so that they would realize the cost was only a few pence per week.

Q **My 11-month-old son wakes at the slightest sound. We usually tiptoe around the flat and whisper, but we can't expect our dinner guests to do the same. Any bright ideas to encourage my son to sleep while we have some fun?**

A Unfortunately, there is no magic cure, although there are all sorts of things worth trying, from lambskins to rocking cradles, from womb music to massage. Having had three children, I sympathize. But it's important at this stage that your son isn't completely dominating your evenings as well as your days. Try to acclimatize him to noise as soon as you can: a good trick is to keep a radio on in his room when he's in bed – I don't mean just soothing music but something like Radio 4 where there'll be adult voices chatting. Start with the volume on low, gradually increasing it night by night, and you should find that he soon copes with sleeping through it. And if you have a second baby, I recommend that as early as possible you start as you mean to go on by getting him used to normal household noise while he sleeps.

Q **I have a perforated ear drum and have never flown before, so would like to know if flying would affect me. I have had different advice from two GPs, so am still searching for the correct information and am unable to book a holiday until I know.**

A

My instinct would be that it's fine, as my daughter had a perforated ear drum as a child and was never prevented from flying. But to be safe I'd check with the Air Travel Advisory Bureau on 020 7636 5000, and BA's Passenger Clearance Unit on 020 8738 5444.

Q

My daughter has just given birth to my first grandchild – in New Zealand. I am overjoyed and long to see her and the baby but I am terrified of flying. The flight is 36 hours long, including a stopover in the Far East and transfer to a domestic flight from Auckland in the north to Christchurch in the south. I am claustrophobic and do not use lifts or the underground, so the prospect of being on a plane for this length of time is so daunting I can barely contemplate it. Have you any idea how I could overcome this problem? Is there any other way of getting to New Zealand?

I do sympathize – you must be having such a struggle between your longing to see them and your fear of getting there, but as there are a few oceans and things between here and New Zealand there's not much doubt that the only two alternatives are to go through the air or over the water. Going by sea is pricey and relies on your having plenty of time on your hands, but you could make it into a wonderful holiday – ask your travel agent for details of round-the-world cruises that would allow you to stop off for a few weeks in Christchurch before heading back to the UK. Sailing time from England is usually around five weeks. The problem is that you're bound to want to visit your grandchild again in the future, and your very understandable fear is always going to prove a barrier. If you can tackle it now then it'll pay off for years to come. A company called Aviatours (01252 793250) run courses led by British Airways pilots that are designed to allay the fears of nervous fliers. They are structured specially for people such as you who have deep-rooted anxieties about flying, including claustrophobia, and they have a high success rate. The course concludes with a 45-minute flight on a BA jet, and most who attend do overcome their fear and prove that they would be able to cope with future flights. The course and flight cost £189, and it could be a very worthwhile investment.

Q My granddaughter has alopecia. Is there a society that could help?

A Losing one's hair at any point in life must be incredibly traumatic but most particularly at her young age. The Alopecia Patients Society is known as Hairline International, and is based at 1668 High Street, Knowle, West Midlands, B93 0LY. If you write to them enclose an A4 size SAE. It is worth contacting them – they have lots to offer.

Q What are your favourite hangover cures?

A If I know at the time I've overdone it, then I do try to drink lots of water before I go to sleep. There's no question that dehydration is a main culprit in causing that horrendous feeling the next morning. I don't always do it: the problem with being a little merry is that water seems so boring at the time. They do say a mug of hot water with a slice of lemon in the morning is helpful, but it is rather virtuous sounding. Otherwise, I think the good old bacon sandwich can't be beaten. It's a good source of carbohydrates if you have thick slices of bread, and low in fat if you choose lean bacon, though actually cereal and toast would be just as good – coupled with some paracetamol and a phone call to apologize for the unnecessary remark that seemed so witty the night before.

Q I suffer terribly from insomnia and have tried everything, from counting sheep to listening to the shipping forecast – all without success. However tired I am, as soon as my head hits the pillow I'm wide awake again. Do you have a magic answer?

A How I wish I did! I'm quite sure, though, that if there were a magic answer we'd all know about it by now, as it's so common. Yes, I too have times when I just can't sleep, and it can be the most frustrating thing in the world. And why is it that little problems seem so frighteningly daunting in the middle of the night? My only tip that may help is that I've found it's important *not* to get up and prowl about, or to listen to the radio or read, much as you may be tempted. I make myself lie there in the dark, trying to empty my head of questions like What is the Meaning of Life, and what was it I meant to put on the shopping list, and concentrate on calming down and telling myself it really doesn't matter if I miss a few hours' sleep. It's not true of course, but if I give in and turn the light on I get into the habit of waking up and find it very hard to break. Some people swear by a new mattress (see page 38).

Q **When you receive a letter out of the blue from a medium claiming that wonderful things are around the corner waiting to happen, and asking for money to reveal all, how do you know if it is genuine? Is there any way you can check up on them?**

A Funnily enough, after reading your letter I had a vision. In this vision a figure, surrounded by an aura of bright light, came unto me and said, 'That medium is a complete phoney and is simply out to make money. The future cannot be foretold. Do not send the cheque.' So now you know.

Q **My girlfriend's small flat has a bad smell because of her cat. She has the litter tray in the kitchen, which I think is very unhygienic. (In a toss up between me and the pet, the cat would win, so please don't suggest getting rid of it.)**

Jane Asher's

A   Meet at your place instead. If that's not possible, tell her about the smell. If the tray is changed often enough and the cat is properly trained, there shouldn't be a problem. And however small the flat, it must surely have a lavatory? Insist the tray moves in there. If you don't sort this out now, your relationship could come up against serious problems later. (Mind you, if the cat really comes first, you might consider keeping an eye out for a girlfriend who has different priorities.)

Q   **I am due to go on holiday to Greece with my boyfriend in a few weeks' time. Two months ago I embarked on a special bikini diet to get rid of my cellulite, but it hasn't worked despite paying out a small fortune on various supposedly slim-lining body lotions. I am so disappointed, as I feel I don't really want to be seen in a swim-suit. I want to cancel the holiday, but my boyfriend says I'm being paranoid. What should I do?**

A   I really can't believe that any of the so-called cellulite-removing lotions make any difference at all: even as a person who can be easily seduced by the claims of various miracle creams of one sort or another, the idea that rubbing some into your thighs can magically dissolve the fatty bits underneath seems too hard to take, especially as most doctors and scientists would deny that 'cellulite' as such actually exists. I fear the unpalatable truth is that to lose weight – from anywhere – the only things that work are less food and more exercise. Don't even think of cancelling your holiday: we all have bits of our bodies that we feel miserable about exposing in swimsuits, but there are lots of ways of – literally – covering our embarrassment. Why not tie a pretty sarong around your hips when you're not actually in the water? You can find bikinis that come with matching ones. Or go for one of the new flattering outfits that come with shorts rather than tiny bikini bottoms. And do remember there's no 'right' size of bottoms and thighs: it's simply a matter of current fashion. Many find a Rubens far more beautiful than a Giacometti. Have a great holiday and don't hold back on the taramasalata and retsina: life's too short to be too sensible.

LIST OF
CONTRIBUTORS

Jane Asher would like to thank the following *Express* readers for their contributions.

Mrs S Abbott, Wigan, Greater
   Manchester
Karen Adams, Stoke-on-Trent
Ali, Colchester
Alison, Newark
Mary Anderson, Midlothian
Andrew, Ilkley, West Yorkshire
Angela, Edinburgh
Anna, Taunton
Mr G T Annabell-Cooper
Annie, London N8
C Anson, Averington
Mrs S Arrow, Essex
Jenny Atter, Lincs
Brenda Baker, Stockport
Mrs Leita Balkwill, Tadworth, Surrey
Mrs J S Ball, Swadlincote, Derbyshire
Peggie Barkham, South Wirral
Mrs Cherrie Bartholomew, West
   Midlands
S Baxter, London N1
Becky, London
Mrs Jean Bell, Kidderminster
Mrs A Bellew, Borehamwood

Betty, Devon
E Billington, Preston, Lancashire
D Blackmore, Northumberland
Shirley Blake, West Yorkshire
Mr and Mrs Bloxham, Oxfordshire
Mrs D R Bone, Southend on Sea
Edith Booth, Warrington
D H Bourne, Redstock
Mrs Pat Bowering, Burton-on-Trent,
   Staffs
Mrs Angela Boyd, Woodhall Spa, Lincs
Amanda Brady, Penryn
Mrs B Braithwaite, Preston
Mrs J M Brett, Wellesbourne,
   Warwickshire
Brian, Edinburgh
Helen Bruce, Maidenhead, Berks
Alodie Bubeck
Mrs K Burton, Farnborough, Hants
D C, Denbighshire, North Wales
Mrs M E Carter, Broadway, Worcs
Caris, London SW3
Caroline, Newcastle
Mrs Anne Carter, Nottinghamshire

Carys, Stafford

Cath, London N10

Cath, Staines

M Celand, Wraysbury, Berks

Mrs Margaret Chapman, Essex

M Cherry, Bognor Regis

Claire, Eastcots, Middlesex

Claire, Kendal

Claire, Manchester

Elaine Clark, Oxted, Surrey

Cynthia Colderick, Swansea

Mr G Conway, Bedworth, Warwks

Mrs L Cook, Nuneaton

Mrs Audrey Corker, Chester

Mrs Marion de Cort, South Benfleet, Essex

A Cory, Camden

Sarah Cottingham, Lund, East Yorkshire

Mrs J B Cregan, Lancashire

Mrs J M Cresswell, Barnsley

Val Crocker, Bishops Stortford

H Crumley, Wokingham, Berks

Brian Cummins

Anne T Curry, Alexandria, Dunbartonshire

L D, Plymouth, Devon

Mrs Peggy Dagnall, Largs, Strathclyde

Mary Dalby, Whitley Bay, Tyne and Wear

Mrs D Dale, Warrington

Miss V E Dale, Twickenham, Middx

Christine Daly, Durham

Damian, Baildon, W Yorks

Danny, Batisford, Suffolk

Mrs Barbara Davies, Devon

Mrs Glenys Davies, Llanelli, Carms

Hazel Dawson, Essex

Mrs M Dayus, Birmingham

Angela Devlin, Rochester, Kent

Mrs E A Dewey, London, NW11

Joan Dix, Woodford

Elizabeth Dixon, Suffolk

Mrs E K Dodsworth, Alcester, Warwickshire

Donald, Nottingham

R E Donaldson, Devon

Dorothy, Harrogate

Mrs D Dowsell, Stroud, Gloucestershire

Pam Driver, York

Mrs Irene Dudley, Southend-on-Sea, Essex

Kathleen Duffield, Saffron Walden

Reg Dunstan, Winchester, Hants

Mrs C Edmunds, Chard, Somerset
W Eley, Lee on Solent, Hants
Tony Elliott, King's Lynn
Valerie Elphee, Paignton, Devon
Emma, Northallerton
Doreen Epps, Kent
Mrs C Eyre, Notts
Mrs Mary Fauckes, Bristol
Mrs Jacqueline Faulkner, Flitwick,
    Bedfordshire
Fiona, Bangor, Wales
Miss E Flynn, Islington, London N1
Mrs Judy Flynn, Wembley
Mrs Christine Food, Sheffield
Jenny Forster, North Wootton,
    Somerset
Catherine Foster, Witney, Oxon
Mrs Pam Fowkes, New Malden, Surrey
K Fowler, Thornhill, Cardiff
Mrs Foxwell, Fulham, London SW6
Amy France, Colchester
Francesca, Knaresborough
C Francis, Plumstead, London SE18
Mrs Betty Frankish, Kingston-upon-
    Hull, East Yorkshire
Milly and Rachel Fry, London SW16
Mrs S E Furber, Sandbach, Cheshire

Mr J Gall, Yeovil
Mr EA Gardner, Surrey
Valerie Gaunt, Cambridge
Deborah Gibbons, Norfolk
Stella Gibson, Paisley
M Gill, Newton Aycliffe, Co Durham
Lorna Gillibrand, Manchester
Mrs Norma Glaswin, Wirral
Glen, Oxford
Mrs Goldsmith, Cosgrove
Mr Peter Goulding, Windlesham
Janette Greenwood, Chesham, Bucks
Dianne Greig, Newark
Mrs Guest, Cornwall
Guy, Leicester
Guy, London W8
T H, Kidderminster
Kate Hallett, Sheen
Nancy Halstead, Wirral
Mrs Hankin, East Sussex
Maureen Harden, Harrow
Chris Hare, St Pancras Housing
    Association, London N1
Shirley Hargy, Ballymoney, Ireland
C Harley, Bedford
Mrs I Harndscombe, Carmarthen
Harriet, Chester

Jane Asher's

N Harris, Devon

Mrs MD Hayward, S Wales

Mrs Freda Healey, Manchester

Mrs O Heggard, Barnstaple

Claire Hellier and Auntie Doris,
Bromsgrove, Worcs

Ruth Henderson, Strood, Kent

Mrs Hendriks-Free, Colchester

Margaret Herbert, Newark,
Nottinghamshire

Mrs C Hewitt, Glasgow

Dawn Higgs, Monmouthshire

J Higham, Southport, Merseyside

Hilary, Leeds

C Hinman, Diss

Elizabeth Holmes, Preston, Lancs

Mrs S Holmes, Newark, Notts

Mrs Hope, Derbyshire

Mrs J M Hoper, Hampshire

June Hopkirk, Lincoln

Barry Horrigan, Dibden Purlieu,
Southampton

Mrs P Horsey, Essex

Maggie Huke, Brentwood

Barbara Humphreys, Devon

Mrs E Hunter, Fife

Irene, Canterbury

B Irwin, Cockermouth

Mrs T Irwin, Huntingdon, Cambs

Isabel, Telford, Shropshire

Patrick James, Hereford

Jane, Newquay

Janet, Southampton

Janice, Bromsgrove

Janice, Guildford, Surrey

Mrs J Jarman, Hants

Jeane, Gloucestershire

Miss E M Jeffrey, Hertfordshire

Juanita Jerrard, Devon

Jill, East Yorkshire

Joan, Frodsham, Cheshire

P M Johnson, Warrington

Mr G Jones, Derbyshire

Mrs J Jones, Mid Glamorgan

Mrs M Jones, Nuneaton

Joy, Dorset

Karina, Ilkley

Kate, Newport

Kathleen, Weymouth

Judith Kelly, Walsall, West Midlands

Mrs J Kemp, Hampstead, London NW3

Jean Kemp, Bristol

Keri, London

A Kitchener, Grantham

C Lander, Fareham, Hampshire

Mrs Brenda Lang, Essex

Mrs B Lawrence, Solihull, West Midlands

Mrs Legg

Pam Leggett, Saxmundham, Suffolk

Angela Lewis, Worcester

Jean Like, Wallingford, Oxon

Lily, Ayrshire

Linda, Hackney

Mrs A Livingstone, Airdrie, Scotland

Nigel Longley, Sale, Cheshire

Lorrie, Leeds

V Lucas, Oxshott, Surrey

K E Luce, Wolverhampton

J M, Rochdale, Lancs

Mrs A McAllister, Ayr, Strathclyde

Henry McDonagh, Bishopbriggs, Glasgow

Patricia MacDonald, Newcastle upon Tyne

Jean McKay, Renfewshire

Sasha McKay, London N1

Maureen McMaster, Kingsley, Cheshire

Mrs G Madin, Pontefract, West Yorkshire

Lynda Maggs, Surrey

Sharon Magill, County Down

Mr J Malcolm, Tayside

Marilyn, St Ives

Marion, Cardiff

Mrs M Markham, Norwich

Mrs Ann Marriott, Grantham, Lincs

Mrs E Marshall, Kent

Mrs Martin, Willersey, Worcs

Mary, Devon

Mary, Wrexham, Clwyd

Jean Mason, Winchmore Hill, London N21

Mrs B Matthews, Banbury, Oxon

Melissa, Kent

Mrs G Merrit, Doncaster

J Michael, Bridport

Michelle, Milton Keynes

Neil Minnot, Nottingham

J Minshull, Warrington

Miranda, Basingstoke

Mrs B Moore, Wakefield

Mrs Josephine Mueller, Peterborough

Mrs R S Murdoch, Suffolk

Mrs Jean Neale, Oxted, Surrey

Mrs J M Nevile, Shipston-on-Stour, Warwickshire

Chris Neville, Redditch

Mrs M Newbold, Bournemouth

Barrie Newby, Reading

Mrs B Niblett, Knutsford

Nicholas, Bangor

Eileen Nolan, Wirral

Ms A Ogden, Rochdale

Mavis Ogden, Flamborough

Olivia, Tiverton

Mrs B O'Rourke, Birmingham

Stuart P, London N1

Mrs S Padgett, Wakefield, Yorks

G Papadopoulos, Bournemouth

Sally Parnell, Jesmond, Newcastle

Mrs Sheila Pashley, Newcastle upon Tyne

Pat, Southampton

Patricia, Hornchurch

Mrs M Pearson, Manchester

Mrs Linda Pendlebury, Croston, Preston

Kate Penn, Oxford

Andrea Perry, Llanfair

Rita Pink, Tunbridge Wells, Kent

Anne Pownall, Peebleshire

Mrs Muriel Price, Chippenham, Wiltshire

Mrs Erica Priddy, Waterlooville

Andrew Putney, London

Mr DB Quine, Cheshire

Mrs Joan Raspin, Grimsby, Lincs

Rebecca, Manchester

Mrs D M Reditt, Essex

James Reid, Glasgow

Mrs Roberts, Wrexham, North Wales

Mrs A Robinson, Preston

David Robinson, Flint

Mrs Janet Rose, Bucks

Ellie Ross, Aylesbury

Mrs Pat Rowe, Ilkeston, Derbyshire

C S, Essex

Penny S, Glasgow

Hazel Sanders, Worcester

Mrs MA Sanders, Nottingham

Mr RS Sandison, Ayrshire

Sarah, Beverley

Sarah, Bristol

Sarah, Huntingdon

L Seaholme, Letchworth, Herts

Jenny Shakespeare, Wetherby, W Yorkshire

Mrs E Sharples, Wigan, Lancs

Miss S V L Shepherd, Wolverhampton

Simon, Newcastle

Mrs J Simons, Bucks

Len Simpson, Poynton
D Smart, Shipley
Mrs A Smith, Inverness-shire
Mrs J M Smith, Farnborough,
    Hants
Jo Smith, Chobham, Surrey
Mr RH Smith, Herne Bay
Jillian Solomon, Rochester, Kent
Sophie, Wendover, Hants
Mrs Vera Southall, Staffs
Rob Speed
Mrs Spike, London
Mr A Steedman, Carnock, Fife
Steve, Liverpool
June Stradling, Burton-on-Trent
Mrs Patricia Strange, Tadcaster, North
    Yorks
Mrs O Sturdy, Maidstone
Susie, Nottingham
Mrs P Suthers, Rochdale, Lancs
Mr T, Derbyshire
J T, Harrow
Mrs B Y Taylor, West Sussex
Mrs Patricia Taylor, Weston Super
    Mare, Somerset
Mrs Vivienne Taylor, Farnborough,
    Hants

Maureen Teasdale, Billingham,
    Stockton Borough
P G Terry, Skipton
Ann Thomas, Cheltenham, Glos
Mrs D Thomas, Swindon
Marie Thornton, Buckhurst Hill, Essex
Mrs Cathy Tilley, Ashburton, Devon
Tim, Tonbridge
Tom, Birmingham
Tony, Selsey, West Sussex
Anne Towner, Edinburgh
Mrs Veronica Tucker, Swindon,
    Wiltshire
Eric Turier, West Sussex
Valerie Usher, Biggleswade
Val, Portsmouth
J Vasey, Brighton
Vicki, Lydd, Kent
Karen Wallace, Edinburgh
Mr G Waller, Torquay
Trish Walsh, Derby
Mrs E Walsham, Colchester
Mrs H O Walton, Powys
Mike Walton
Mrs Muriel Ward, Leicester
Mary Warner, Southampton
Mrs G Watson, Garforth, Leeds

Jane Asher's

Wayne, Ipswich

Mrs Gisella Webzell, Gravesend,
Kent

Mr D R Wedge, Herts

Ruth Wells, Colne

Wendy, Glasgow

Jennifer Weston, Ely, Cambridgeshire

Mr R W Wharton, Inverkeithing, Fife

C Wheater, London SW7

Pippa Wheeler, Mordiford,
Herefordshire

Mrs Whittingham, Mid Glamorgan

Mrs J Widdowson, Barnsley

June Wilkinson, Stafford

Mrs D Williams, Manchester

Mrs Barbara Wilson, Clackmannan

Mrs J Wilson, Waterloo, Merseyside

Mrs C Wiltshire, Hastings

Mrs B Withall, Hitchen

Mary Wrighton, Essex

Celia Wyatt, Ashford, Middlesex

Wyn, Wiltshire

D E Y, Birmingham

A Yates, Alton

INDEX

This index is not a comprehensive listing of all and every item and topic covered in the book – it would be a book in itself! – but instead is designed to be a guide to help you find the subject area you are looking for. For example, if you wish to find out about French polishing, try under 'Renovations'.